A Simple Plant-Based Diet Eating Guide For The Middle Aged

Whole-food Plant-Based Diet Guide For Beginners| Exclusive Guide to a Vegan Diet| Menus To Improve Your Athletic Performance and Sex life

Edyth J. Garson

INTRODUCTION

Congratulations for purchasing this book.

The latest trend in the diet industry is plant-based diets. These diets are particularly effective for losing weight and living a healthier life, making them ideal for the middle-aged who find health problems such as obesity, heart disease, and type 2 diabetes. But going on a completely new diet can be daunting and complicated. This ebook breaks down the various plant-based diets, explains them, and provides simple, easy-to-follow diet plans for getting started. From there, you will also find how a plant-based diet can improve your athletic performance brainpower. You'll also learn how to spice up things in your bedroom by eating plant-based foods, how plant-based foods can affect your mental health, and also how plant foods affect the environment.A Plant-Based Diet is a great way to improve your health in middle age. It can be a lifelong lifestyle for most people. Some people can begin eating a plant-based diet immediately. Others must take the process in steps. A gradual transition will result in greater health in the long run. You can incorporate a vegan or vegetarian diet into your daily life.

CHAPTER ONE: INTRODUCTION TO PLANT-BASED DIETS

What is a Plant-Based Diet? The short answer: it's a way of eating where your food mainly consists of plants. This includes not only fruits and vegetables but also nuts, seeds, oils, whole grains, legumes, and beans. It doesn't mean that you are vegetarian or vegan and never eat meat or dairy. Rather, you are proportionately choosing more of your foods from plant sources.

What are the Types of Plant-Based Diets Available?

There are many plant-based diets, but most people are only familiar with a few. Some of these diets are for people at risk for chronic diseases such as heart disease, but others may not be what you're looking for. The good news is that you can experiment with various options until you find one that works best for you. Here are the types of plant-based diets that you need to note.

01.Mediterranean Diet

The Mediterranean diet is a flavorful and healthy way of eating based on the traditional foods found in countries bordering the Mediterranean Sea. French, Spanish, Greek, and Italian cuisine are all based on healthy ingredients like fruits, vegetables, whole grains, and heart-healthy fats like olive oil. And because fish, seafood, dairy, and poultry are included in moderation, it's a balanced way to eat. Red meat and sweets are eaten only occasionally, so you can enjoy them without overindulging.

 Olive oil provides the bonus for lowering bad LDL cholesterol while raising good HDLs (the type we need). Fish/seafood can be consumed without worrying about high sodium content. They're generally cooked using milder spices such as olive oil so it doesn't overpower your meal like others may think when dining on this type of diet. In addition, dairy products make up only one percent but still provide many benefits, including calcium intake throughout all ages.

02. Flexitarian Diet

This diet, created by Dawn Jackson Blatner, enables people to reap the benefits of vegetarian eating while enjoying animal products in moderation. It is also known as the Semi-vegetarian diet. People following this diet are primarily vegetarian, consuming lots of fruits, vegetables, whole grains, beans, nuts, seeds, and legumes, including a small amount of meat, poultry, fish, and seafood. They might include dairy foods and eggs, depending on personal preference. This flexible type of eating is an excellent starting point that will allow you more flexibility when it comes time to start incorporating plant-based meals into your everyday life!

03. Whole-food Plant-based Diet (WFPB)

A whole-food, plant-based diet is more of a lifestyle than a specific diet. The term "whole" in WFPB describes foods that are minimally processed. It focuses on eating mostly plants, including vegetables, fruits, whole grains, legumes, seeds, and nuts. Processed foods, like heavily refined grain products, foods with added sugars or artificial sweeteners, and foods with added fat are not included in a WFPB diet. This means avoiding these types of foods as much as possible.

04. Vegetarian Diet

Just as there are different types of plant-based diets, there are many different types of vegetarian diets. They vary from the more restrictive vegetarian options like the Vegan diet to the less restrictive options like Pescatarian and Semi-vegetarian diet. They include:

- **Pescatarian**: Someone who eats fish and seafood, dairy, eggs, and honey but eliminates all meat and poultry from their diet.
- **Lacto-Ovo Vegetarian**: Someone who eats dairy, eggs, and honey but eliminates all animal flesh (meat, poultry, fish, seafood).
- **Lacto-vegetarian**: Eats dairy and honey but eliminates all other animal products.
- **Ovo-vegetarian:** Eat eggs and honey but eliminate all other animal products.

- **Vegan**: Eliminates all animal products, including honey (the word vegan implies these dietary changes are ethical despite the term vegan being used in other ways).

Why Do Some People Make The Switch To A Plant-Based Lifestyle?

A plant-based diet is becoming increasingly popular for several reasons. Some people switch because they want to improve their health and feel better, some do it to lose weight, and others do it because they care about animals or the environment. Whatever your reason may be, we're going to talk about why you should consider making the switch too!

One of the best things about a plant-based diet is that it's so healthy. Many people make the switch because they're looking for a way to improve their health, and a plant-based diet delivers. Plant-based diets are low in saturated fat and cholesterol, and they're high in fiber, vitamins, and minerals. Because plant-based diets are also high in antioxidants and phytochemicals, they may even help reduce the risk of cancer and heart disease! Remember that not all plant-based diets are healthy. Your market is probably flooded with processed plant-based foods. Well, these processed options will do more harm than good to your health.

A second reason why some people make the switch is to lose weight. Many people struggle with their weight, but switching over to a healthy diet like this can help them get back on track. Plant-based foods may also help you maintain your weight in the long run because they are made up of lots of fiber-rich foods and exclude consumption of processed foods. In addition, many plant-based foods are rich in fruits and vegetables, which contribute to satiety. Research indicates that individuals eating a vegetarian diet have lower body weights than those who eat meat.

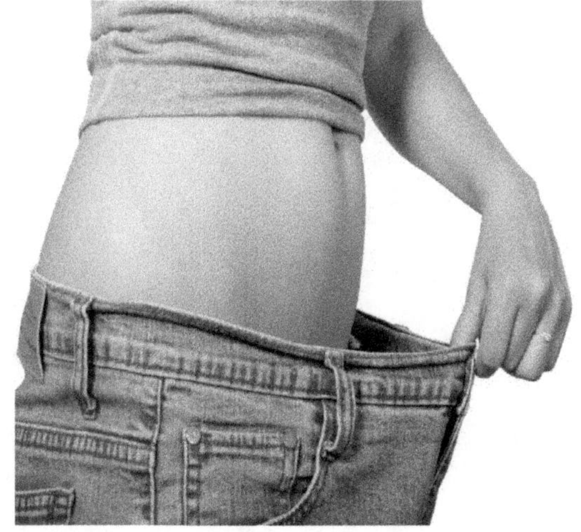

Eating a balanced, whole-food plant-based diet may also help with weight loss for people trying to lose weight through calorie restriction. This has been demonstrated in numerous studies looking at calorie-restricted plant-based diets. All these can help you with the health problems of being overweight and obese. Still, the plant-based group also showed improvements in heart disease risk factors such as cholesterol levels and blood pressure!

Finally, some choose to go plant-based because they care about animals or the environment. Eating a healthy, plant-based diet is not only good for your health, it's also extremely important when it comes to living sustainably. From land use and resource allocations to the amount of pollution created by industrial-scale agricultural businesses, what you put in your mouth has a dramatic effect on the environment surrounding us all. So if you care about the death and destruction of animal farming operations across the globe as well as having a respectable impact on our planet for generations to come, then plant-based or whole foods are for you! Factory farming is one of the leading causes of climate change, so by choosing a plant-based diet, you're doing your part to help the environment. And as we all know, factory farming also leads to animal abuse and mistreatment, so by going plant-based, you're also helping animals!

Why Is A Plant-Based Diet Good For You?

A plant-based diet is based on foods derived from plants, including vegetables, fruits, legumes, grains, nuts, and seeds. In the form of its raw state, fruits and vegetables also provide a great source of fiber. Even studies indicate that eating more fiber may help you lose weight. Incorporating more fruits and vegetables into your diet can help you reduce your risk of many different diseases. Most diets focus on cutting calories and losing weight, but you'll achieve much more if you go for a healthy diet that focuses on incorporating vegetables and fruits into your daily meals. The benefits of eating a plant-based diet are cumulative. A diet that cuts back on meat and animal products may not sound like it's going to be the best way to eat, but after some time, you'll start to see all the amazing health benefits of eating a plant-based diet. If you haven't done so already, it might be a good idea to look into vegetarianism. Studies indicate that people who consume meat every day are at a greater risk of developing cancer and heart disease. Additionally, plant-based diets can help you feel better both mentally and physically. Here are a few reasons (Science-Based) why you should consider switching to a plant-based diet:

I.   **Plant-Based Diets Provide Your Body With Vital Nutrients.**

I worked in a refugee camp when I was doing voluntary work. The faces of malnourished children that I interacted with can give someone goosebumps. Well, the reality of life is that many people can't afford the basic nutrients that you need for an active and healthy life. Plant-based diets are often rich in fiber, antioxidants, and other healthy compounds that may help protect against chronic disease. They also provide more potassium than traditional meat-based eating habits do; this makes them great for the heart! But if you go without any animal products at all - like "veganism" or even just being vegetarian -- your body will still need plenty of calcium, too, because dairy products provide an excellent source of vitamin D within our bodies when consumed regularly over time.

II.   **Plant-Based Diets Can Help You Lose Weight.**

Have you ever been called a 'pig'? Well, that's what I encountered when I was in high school. Being body shamed repeatedly inspired me to study nutrition in college. My close friends persuaded me to hit the gym, but I found myself going to McDonald's every time I got out of the gym. This made my life worse than before. Ever since I started studying nutrition, I found that matters of weight loss start in the kitchen and end in the kitchen!

Many different types of plant-based diets can be used to lose weight. One type, veganism, is the most preferred. Observational studies show vegans are thinner than those who don't follow this dietary tradition. Still, there is also substantial evidence from controlled experiments—the gold standard in scientific research--supporting its effectiveness.

Plants vs. Zombies might sound like an interesting game, but it's based on how well one can avoid eating them! The average American eats about 18 billion fast-food calories per year. Most contain high amounts of fat or sugar, which are not good if one wants to maintain healthy lifestyle habits into adulthood.

III. Plant-Based Diets Can Lower Your Blood Sugar Levels and Improve Your Kidney Function.

There's a reason why people with diabetes tend to follow plant-based eating. Not only are they more effective at reducing blood sugar levels and preventing further medical issues, but some studies report this even more so than diets recommended in ADA or National Cholesterol Education Program guidelines!

A plant-based diet can help you manage your type 2 diabetes via reduced appetite, which has been shown in clinical trials as one way it reduces HbA1C (a long-term measure for monitoring how well someone regulates their blood sugar). You also get plenty of extra fiber from grains like quinoa or amaranth - not to mention all those veggies—which protect against chronic illnesses.

IV. Plant-Based Diets have been Linked to Reduced Risks of Certain Types of Cancer.

Mods may not be as popular now, but they were once the go-to for anyone looking to make their car sound better. Plant-based diets such as Veganism have been linked with a reduced risk of cancer in several studies. Researchers believe that this may be because vegans generally consume more legumes, fruits, and vegetables than those who don't follow a vegan diet. Vegans have a 15% lower chance of developing or dying from cancer. Eating legumes regularly may help you have a 9-18% reduced rate for colorectal or stomach cancers than nonvegetarians.

Research shows that those who eat seven servings per day are less likely (15%) to develop an aggressive type of prostate tumor called adenocarcinoma compared with people watching their diet.

V. Plant-Based Diets are Linked to a Lower Risk of Heart Disease.

Vegan diets are much better for your heart than you might think! Several studies have shown that these plant-based eating plans can reduce blood sugar and bad LDL cholesterol levels by 46%. What's more, reducing hypertension placed on a reduced calorie intake may help prevent organs from becoming damaged over time.

So go ahead - indulge without fear when it comes to what we put into our bodies because if there were ever an argument against meat consumption, then this would surely do duty nicely.

It's true: vegan food tastes great AND keeps us healthy!

VI. A Plant-Based Diet Will Improve Your Gut Health.

Did you know that a healthy gut microbiome promotes high-functioning metabolism and a strong immune system? Did you know that it can also support the development of appropriate levels of hormones that contribute to appetite regulation and promote healthy bowel movements and even your mood? So how can a plant-based diet help you promote a healthy gut? Well, the beneficial bacteria in your gut microbiota ferment fiber to feed themselves. These 'good' microorganisms take up space and resources in your gut, making it hard for pathogenic bacteria to survive. This means a fiber-rich diet filled with fruits, vegetables, whole grains, and legumes can be very beneficial for your microbiota.

VII. A Plant-Based Diet Can Help You Reduce Inflammation.

Inflammation is the body's natural response to fight off any invader that comes into contact with it. It can be caused by a splinter, an irritant (like allergies), or pathogens such as bacteria and viruses - but in cases where there are autoimmune diseases onboard, your immune system attacks healthy tissue instead! All these factors have been shown time again how they affect inflammation levels.

Healthy diets, including vegan and vegetarian ones, can provide many health benefits, including reducing inflammation. These diets are packed with phytochemicals, including antioxidants, flavonoids, and carotenoids, all of which help reduce inflammation and protect tissues from damage. Several of these phytochemicals have anti-inflammatory properties. Antioxidants are well-known for their cancer-fighting abilities, but they also reduce inflammation by preventing the overproduction of inflammatory chemicals.

Foods high in zinc, including pumpkin seeds, nuts, and beans, can reduce inflammation associated with asthma and other respiratory conditions. Omega-3 fatty acids are found in fish, flaxseeds, seaweed, and leafy greens, like spinach and kale. Most spices and herbs can be anti-inflammatory. And, the more color in your diet, the better.

These include red peppers, apples, berries, citrus fruits, dark leafy greens, and other brightly colored vegetables. Carotenoids, lutein, and zeaxanthin may help prevent inflammation as they are found in green leafy vegetables, tomatoes, and carrots.

VIII.   Plant-Based Diets Can Improve Your Athletic Performance.

Athletes train more rigorously than the average person and regularly push their bodies to their limits, especially if they are involved in physically demanding sports. As such, they must fuel their bodies with nourishing food. A Plant-Based Diet is a great choice for athletes because it boosts energy and improves athletic performance. In addition, a plant-based diet can help you recover from an intense workout faster and minimize sickness.

A plant-based diet is a perfect diet for athletes and others who want to get in shape. It's important to note that it is not a short-term goal. This diet is a lifestyle change for those who want to get fit and lose weight. It is important to find a diet that works for you and is compatible with your goals. A plant-based diet is the best option for athletes looking to achieve their fitness goals.

A plant-based diet is not only good for your heart, but it can also help you feel more energized and stay healthy. The anti-inflammatory principles of plants benefit athletes in major ways as they recover from workouts or injuries sustained during competition time.

Tennis pro-Venus Williams found that a vegan lifestyle allowed her to manage an autoimmune disease called Sjögren's syndrome without prescription medications. At the same time, tennis Commentator Mary Carillo transitioned towards eating healthier when she overcame food allergies which gave rise to eczema on both hands after taking medication designed specifically to treat one symptom instead of addressing all symptoms.

Biggest Concerns About a Plant-Based Diet: All the Myths Busted!

You've probably heard of people going vegan or vegetarian and perhaps thought to yourself, "They'll never get enough protein! " or "You're kidding! I thought I could eat whatever I wanted as long as it was plant-based. How come I can't eat some plant foods?" Well, maybe you were right, or maybe you were wrong. So, it's time to get the facts!

1) A Plant-Based Diet Is Deficient In Protein.

Animal-based proteins contain all the essential amino acids, while plant-based proteins lack one or more. To ensure you're getting all the protein you need, make sure you're eating a variety of plants that supply the appropriate quantity and combination of amino acids. Eating a variety of plant-based foods is enough to give you the Recommended Daily Allowance (RDA) of nutrients that you need for an active and healthy life.

2) Plant-Based Diet Is Deficient In Certain Nutrients

Plant-based diets can be deficient in certain nutrients, such as iron. Although plant-based sources offer you some protection against anemia and deficiency problems by providing vitamin C, which helps absorb calcium more easily, or Vitamin B12 found naturally within foods like meat products.

It's also important not to forget about the importance of adding supplements if needed since plants don't contain Vitamin B12, which means that without these additions, a person could develop anemia from lack thereof-so eat plenty of soy products like fortified soy milk along with nutritional yeast so they'll last throughout their day.

3) Starting A Plant-Based Diet Requires More Planning and Preparation.

There are endless plant-based recipes, but most people did not grow up learning them. This can make it more difficult for those who are just starting. However, with a little creativity, it's easy to find recipes that are both delicious and nutritious. Then, when you're starting a plant-based lifestyle, it's not like you're going to overhaul everything in your kitchen, no! You'll start by making small modifications to the meals you already enjoy. Like you can start by adding more veggies to your meat. That doesn't require more planning doesn't it?

4) Some Plant-Based Foods May Be "Hard To Find"

The first concern is that whole food is often unavailable in many places. This is especially true in places where meat is widely available. Moreover, many restaurants do not offer much choice for plant-based menus. So, the only solution is to purchase fortified foods. Thankfully, this is easier said than done.

5) Plant-Based Diets May Be Expensive

When people think about a plant-based diet, they automatically assume it's expensive. However, this isn't always the case! It's possible to follow a plant-based diet in a very affordable, efficient way. Whether you're a vegetarian or a vegan, it's possible to stay on a budget. It's merely a matter of what kind of budget you're working with and how quickly you want to change your habits. It would be best to focus on plant-based staples and then purchase additional items that can be added to those staples.

There are many ways to eat a plant-based diet. Keep in mind that what you'll want to focus on a plant-based diet is minimally processed foods, so your ice cream, cheeses, and salad dressings aren't what you're going for here. As for fruits and vegetables, these can be purchased from farmer's markets when they're in season because they'll be more costly during the off-season at the grocer.

It's just like produce that comes to us during holiday seasons - they're crazy expensive! So like any other kind of shopping, make sure you know when things are at their best price rather than splurging at the wrong time!

6) Plant-Based Diets Can Be Restrictive

I remember having a difficult time cutting out meat in my diet. I struggled to know where to get my plant-based proteins. Well, you may be struggling with the same problem.

Adopting a plant-based diet took some getting used to at first. But now, I love it. It feels like a whole world of options is available to me at my fingertips. You see, plant-based meats can be replaced by things like mushrooms and tofu in dishes. Cheese alternatives can be homemade with nuts and spices blended. Even date-sweetened desserts don't rely on sugar or syrup bases! Get comfortable taste-testing different vegetables, fruits, legumes, and grains so that you experiment with what works best for you. Recently I tried using roasted Brussels sprouts in a creamy Dijon dressing dish. If I'd never tried such a thing before, I wouldn't have believed how delicious it could be! Be adventurous when experimenting!

7) A Plant-Based Diet Will Make You Lose Muscle

Some people believe that a plant-based diet may damage muscle. If you love fitness and even compete, you care deeply about your muscle growth and physical performance. Protein is an important building block for body tissues, including muscle, regardless of the source. In other words, the consumption of protein-rich plant foods can as effectively build muscle as animal-based foods. So feel free to eat nuts, seeds, and legumes!

8) A Plant-Based Diet Isn't Satisfying.

My sister hasn't been a fan of a plant-based diet. Well, I took several months to convince her to try this lifestyle, and she took years to fully transition to a plant-based diet! One of her reasons for not adopting a plant-based diet early was that she thought she wouldn't get full after eating plant-based foods. My sister eats a lot, so it was hard convincing her that plant-based foods are equally satisfying as animal-based foods.

Regarding their diets, many people express anxiety regarding shifts away from the norm. Their reasoning? A lot of this stems from the fear of being hungry.

Because plant-based food is often low in calorie density, it's likely to leave you feeling unsatisfied at first. However, fruits, vegetables, whole grains, and legumes are also high in fiber — which will leave you feeling full for longer — so there shouldn't be much cause for concern!

9) You Won't Get Complete Proteins from a Plant-Based Diet Unless You Combine Specific Foods

Completing proteins isn't just a mealtime necessity for vegetarians and vegans. When you eat legumes, grains, nuts, and seeds with every meal, your body will naturally combine them to create complete proteins. Of course, many of us make room in our diets for more obvious protein sources — like chicken, fish, or beef — but we should be careful not to overlook plant-based foods rich in protein. For example, a half-cup of lentils provides 18 percent of the recommended daily allowance of protein. So keep eating those beans on salads, mashed into soups, and blended into smoothies!

10) Kids Aren't a Fan of Vegetables.

I wasn't a fan of vegetables when I was young. This was mainly because I only knew that Kale and Spinach were available. My bad!

When veggies like cauliflower, Brussels sprouts, spinach, and artichokes are cooked for kids in a way that makes them taste good, they gobble them up—and kids who do so tend to enjoy eating their vegetables even more. Why not get your little ones involved in the cooking process? They're likely to eat their greens more easily if they've helped out with picking out specific vegetables and deciding what they want to do with them while you're preparing dinner together.

11) Plant-Based Diet Makes You 100% Healthy.

Not all plant-based foods are healthy. Plant-based foods can come in many different forms, and the way they are processed makes a huge difference in the nutritional value you receive from consuming them. Many health professionals agree that a diet consisting primarily of minimally processed fruits, vegetables, legumes, and grains is best for your physical wellbeing. Still, not all plant-based foods fall into that category.

When an ingredient is heavily processed, many beneficial nutrients could be stripped away. For example, French fries, potato chips, cupcakes, and sugary cereals are plant-based. Still, they aren't generally recognized as the best option when looking at them regarding their impact on our health and wellbeing.

12) Plant-Based Diets Don't Give You Strong Bones Like Dairy.

There's this misconception that milk is the source of calcium. Well, Milk is the most well-known source of calcium, but it's far from the only one! A good tip here is to go beyond dairy - there are plenty of other plant-based options available, including leafy greens like kale and mustard greens, as well as fortified fruit juices like orange juice and soy milk.

13) Going Plant-Based Means, I Cut Off Meat Forever.

To say that going plant-based means you stop eating meat would be a gross oversimplification of this dietary lifestyle. The reality is that being part of the plan and making vegetables the main focus of your diet sure does open up plenty of room for many different options, and one example happens to be meat. People with plant-based diets mostly eat plants and plant-based foods like fruits, vegetables, grains, nuts, and seeds, and some may also include meat because that's sort of how it works - one is reducing their overall intake of animal products but not eliminating them unless you go Vegan. One way of reducing your meat intake is by trying the famous "Meatless Mondays."

CHAPTER TWO: TIPS FOR STARTING A PLANT-BASED LIFESTYLE

Here Are The Tips I've Personally Used To Help Me Make The Switch To A Plant-Based Diet. Why Don't You Make The Switch Too?

It's often hard to find the motivation to go plant-based, but it's a pretty easy lifestyle to follow once you do it. Whether you want to lose weight, feel better or stop contributing to animal cruelty, this is a move that could hugely benefit your life. It can take some willpower to get started, but it'll be easy and painless if you use these tips.

Tip 1: You can start any time or day.

It's never too late to start a plant-based diet. Starting a plant-based diet is a great way to improve your health and wellbeing. You can start any time or day - there's no need to wait! You may be 20 years old, or 40 or even 60 yrs. Let me tell you that there's no specific age that you must have for you to change to a plant-based diet. You can adopt the plant-based diet even right now! A plant-based diet is a great way to get your daily dose of fruits and vegetables, and it's also a great way to reduce your risk of chronic diseases. So why wait? Start your plant-based journey today!

Tip 2: Please keep it simple. Don't over-complicate it.

Remember the baby steps you used to make when you were a kid? Apply them here too! A plant-based diet is simple to follow, but that doesn't mean it's easy. It takes more time to shop, prepare and eat plant-based foods than a standard diet, but if you make it simple, you'll have no trouble eating healthier! Here are a few tips to keep your plant-based diet simple: Set the scene - this is what you're looking for. Don't spend your time cooking, but spend your time eating healthier!

Tip 3: Find your favorites.

Developing a plant-based diet is an exciting step, but getting started is not easy. Have you tried countless recipe books and recipes on the internet? In the process, you've probably come across countless vegan recipes that sound delicious but end up disappointing. There's no need to fear! It can be hard to find the perfect recipe, but it's also easy to develop a collection of your favorite plant-based recipes. (Keep in mind: once you develop a collection of favorites, they can become your go-to meals.) You can start by working through the recipes - This is where you'll save time and money. Instead of buying many vegan products only to find out, you don't use them, try cooking with what you already have in your kitchen and develop recipes that use those ingredients. Go through the recipes you love and ask yourself, "What could I add to make this recipe my favourite?" - Most likely, you already have the ingredients in your pantry or fridge. Give a recipe a try and then move on to another one - You may want to start by adding a new ingredient to your favorite recipes. Before you get too far along, look over your recipes and see if any you've tried have multiple variations.

Tip 4: Where do you get plant proteins?

Animal-based foods such as meat, poultry, milk, and fish are some complete protein sources. You have to incorporate a variety of plant-based foods throughout the day to get the complete proteins from plant-based sources. So, where do you get your plant-based proteins from?

- Many legumes are packed with protein, such as lentils, beans, peas, edamame/soybeans (and products made from soy: tofu, tempeh, etc.), and peanuts. These delicious and nutritious foods are packed with protein, making them an important part of any plant-based diet.
- A nutritious and protein-packed snack option, nuts and seeds like almonds, cashews, and walnuts are a great way to fuel your body. Hazelnuts, pecans, hemp seeds, pumpkin seeds, sunflower seeds, flax seeds, sesame seeds, and chia seeds are also great protein sources.
- Whole grains with protein? Kamut, Teff, Wheat, Quinoa, Rice, Wild Rice, Millet, Oats, and Buckwheat have you covered!
- Corn, broccoli, asparagus, brussels sprouts, and artichokes are some examples of vegetables and fruits that contain higher protein levels than other plant-based foods.

Tip 5: Get the right sources of carbohydrates.

On average, people need 1,800 to 2,000 calories per day. A plant-based diet is key to maintaining energy and stamina throughout the day. By incorporating complex carbohydrates into your diet, you can ensure that you have the sustained energy you need to perform at your best. Carbs should be your main energy source, so always focus on eating complex carbs rather than simple carbs.

Complex carbs (such as whole grains, vegetables, and legumes) are slowly digested by the body and provide sustained energy throughout the day. Simple carbs (like white bread, sweets, and processed foods) digest quickly and often result in a blood sugar spike that leads to fatigue and energy crashes.

Tip 6: Know the right sources Plant-Based Fats

Good fats are important for keeping your organs functioning properly, having healthy skin, and hair, and helping your body absorb important vitamins. The three main types of dietary fats include; unsaturated, saturated, and trans fats. Saturated fats are typically solid at room temperature. Most nutrition experts recommend limiting saturated fat intake to prevent an imbalance that can lead to harmful Low Density Lipoprotein (LDL) cholesterol and blockages in arteries. Sources of saturated fat include red meat, whole milk, cheese, coconut oil, and commercially prepared baked goods. Trans fats are a type of unhealthy fat found in dairy products and meats. However, they are also often found in hydrogenated vegetable oils and processed foods. Trans fats raise LDL (bad cholesterol) levels while lowering the High Density Lipoprotein (HDL) commonly referred to as the "good cholesterol." Additionally, trans fats are associated with a higher risk of heart disease, obesity, and type 2 diabetes. Unsaturated fats, on the other hand, can have beneficial effects on your body by decreasing LDL ("bad") cholesterol and increasing HDL ("good") cholesterol levels.

There are many different types of omega-3 fatty acids, but alpha-linolenic acid (ALA) is the only one that is essential- you can only get it from your diet. The long-chain omega-3 fatty acids, EPA and DHA, are not essential, but they do have many health benefits, so it's a good idea to include them in your diet whenever possible. The American Heart Association recommends limiting your daily fat intake to 25-35% of total calories and saturated fat to less than 7% of total calories for heart health. Aim for the following foods for your plant-based protein:

- **Nuts**

You've probably gone nuts when someone annoyed you. But, there's also the good nuts that you should go for. They won't make you angry or hungry for sure. Adding nuts to your diet is a great way to get healthy fats and minerals into your body. Walnuts, almonds, pistachios, and pecans are great sources of monounsaturated and polyunsaturated fats, omega-3 and omega-6 fatty acids, and other minerals. Brazil nuts and cashews are also great sources of fat.

- **Avocados**

Avocados are a nutritional powerhouse, providing a creamy, delicious way to add healthy fats to your diet. With 77% fat, most of it is monounsaturated; they're a great way to boost your nutrient intake. One medium avocado provides 21 grams of fat and vitamins, minerals, and antioxidants.

- **Coconut**

Coconut and coconut oil are a source of medium-chain triglycerides (MCTs). MCTs are a type of saturated fat that is easier for the liver to break down and convert into energy or ketones. MCTs help curb hunger, keep you satiated for longer, and reduce calorie consumption.

- **Flaxseeds**

Flax Seeds are a great source of plant-based omega3 fatty acids. In just one tablespoon, you can get up to 1.8 grams of omega 3s. Add them to your favorite smoothie, granola bars, or morning oats for a healthy and delicious crunch.

- **Extra Virgin Olive Oil**

Extra-virgin olive oil is a nutritional powerhouse, providing a rich source of polyunsaturated fatty acids, including omega-6 and omega-3 fatty acids. A single tablespoon of this healthful oil packs in 14 grams of fat, making it a valuable addition to any diet.

Tip 7: Know the Minerals and vitamins you need for a healthy life.

- **Vitamin B12**

Vitamin B12 is a water-soluble vitamin not found in any plant food. Vitamin B12 is required for healthy nervous system function, proper energy levels, red blood cell formation, and more. An adequate intake of B12 is important for the optimal functioning of the central nervous system and the immune system. The body also requires Vitamin B12 for red blood cell formation and proper DNA synthesis. You can get your daily dose of vitamin B12 from many vegan-friendly foods fortified with nutrients, such as plant milk, soy products, and breakfast cereals. Additionally, Vitamin B12 supplements are a great way to ensure you're getting enough of the nutrient. Those who don't follow strict plant-based eating like the vegan diet, fish, dairy products, eggs, meat, and poultry are excellent animal sources of vitamin B12.

You only need 2.4 micrograms of vitamin B12 each day, but pregnant or breastfeeding teens and women need more - 2.6 to 2.8 mcg daily.

- **Vitamin D**

Vitamin D is a fat-soluble vitamin that is important for optimal health, including promoting healthy bones and teeth and the proper function of the immune system. You can get Vitamin D from the sun, but it's also found in foods. This vitamin is found in some plant-based foods like mushrooms, fortified foods, and fortified milk. But be careful with your intake of vitamin D supplements since this can cause a condition called hypervitaminosis D. Fish, offal, egg, dairy products, and meat are some animal sources of vitamin D. The best way to get your daily dose of vitamin D is by taking 400 international units (IU) if you are 12 months or younger, 600 IU if you are between the ages of 1 and 70, and 800 IU if you are over 70.

- **Iron**

Iron is essential for proper energy production, oxygen transportation, and red blood cell formation, among other things. It is best obtained through plant-based foods or supplements. Good sources of iron include beans, lentils, mushrooms, fortified milk, tofu, and dark green leafy vegetables. Red meats, poultry, offal, fish, eggs are some animal sources of iron. Too little iron can leave you exhausted and decrease your immune function due to anemia.

Adult men and post-menopausal women need only 8 mg of iron per day. 18 mg is the recommended dose for adult women, and pregnant women should shoot for 27 mg per day.

There are two types of iron: heme and non-heme. Heme iron is only found in animal products, while non-heme iron is found in plants. Your body more easily absorbs heme iron than non-heme iron. Some people recommend that vegans aim for 1.8 times the normal RDA, but more studies are needed to establish whether high intakes are necessary.

- **Zinc**

Zinc is essential for proper immune system function, brain and nervous system development, wound healing, growth and development of teeth and bones, reproduction, and more. This mineral is found in fortified foods, whole grains, beans, nuts, and legumes. Oysters, red meat, and poultry are some animal sources of zinc. Zinc is a mineral that is essential in small amounts but can have adverse effects when taken in high doses for long periods. These can include suppressed immunity, decreased HDL levels, anemia, and copper deficiency. You should aim to consume 8 milligrams of zinc per day if you're a woman and 11 milligrams if you're a man.

- **Calcium**

Calcium is important for proper energy production, muscle contraction, blood clotting, and neurotransmitter and hormone production. It is found in fortified foods such as tofu, kale, broccoli, collard greens, legumes, seeds, and grains.

Some supplements may contain calcium as well. Canned sardines and salmon with bones are some animal sources of calcium. According to WHO, 500 to 700 mg of calcium per day is recommended.

- **Potassium**

Potassium is important for proper bodily functions and muscle contraction. It is found in fruits and vegetables and some fortified foods like potato products. Fish, poultry, and meats can provide calcium too.

Despite the lack of an RDA for potassium, many organizations recommend consuming at least 3,500 mg per day through food.

- **Iodine**

Getting enough iodine is crucial for healthy thyroid function, which controls your metabolism. Without enough iodine, you may develop hypothyroidism (low thyroid function). Symptoms of hypothyroidism include fatigue, brain fog, weight gain, and hair loss.

Foods with high iodine levels are iodized salt, seafood, seaweed, and dairy products. Vegans not getting enough iodine from seaweed or iodized salt should consider taking an iodine supplement. The RDA for iodine is 150 mcg per day for adults. If you're pregnant, you should aim for 220 mcg per day. Those breastfeeding are recommended to further increase their daily intake to 290 mcg per day. Children aged 1 to 3 years old should have 90 mcg of iodine per day, while those aged 4 to 8 should have 130 mcg.

- **Vitamin C (Ascorbic acid)**

The nutrient you need for strong bones and healthy muscles is Vitamin C. This vitamin is essential for healing wounds and forming new tissue. Many plant-based foods are good sources of vitamin C, including lemons, grapefruits, cantaloupe, spinach, red peppers, broccoli, tomatoes, kiwi, blackberries, and strawberries. Vitamin C is also found in fortified foods such as orange juice and fruits. Though vitamin C is not found in high quantities in cooked animal foods, it can still be acquired through other means. Raw liver, fish roe, and eggs are all great sources of nutrients and raw meat and fish.

Adult Recommended Daily Amount of Vitamin C is 65-90 milligrams. The upper limit is 2000 milligrams.

- **Vitamin A**

Vitamin A is key for keeping your vision healthy, keeping your immune system and organs functioning properly, and aiding in the growth and development of babies in the womb. There are many plant-based sources of Vitamin A beyond meat, eggs, fish, and dairy products. Examples include tomatoes, papaya, red peppers, spinach, kale, sweet potatoes, butternut squash, carrots, and cantaloupe.

Adult men and women need 900 and 700 micrograms of vitamin A each day, respectively.

- **Vitamin E**

Vitamin E is an essential nutrient for overall health. It supports the immune system, helps cells regenerate, and has antioxidant and anti-inflammatory properties. Vitamin E is found in all sorts of delicious plant-based foods, such as almonds, beet greens, collard greens, spinach, avocado, mango, and more! Shrimp, octopus, crayfish, and lobster are some animal sources of Vitamin E.

Adults need at least 15 milligrams of vitamin E each day to stay healthy.

- **Vitamin K**

Known as the clotting vitamin, vitamin K is key in blood clotting and bone metabolism. This fat-soluble vitamin is essential for the body to produce prothrombin, a necessary protein for blood clotting. There are two types of vitamin K: vitamin K1 and vitamin K2. Vitamin K1 is mainly found in plant-based foods, while vitamin K2 is only found in animal-based and fermented plant foods. A daily value of 120 mcg is recommended. Some of the best plant-based sources of Vitamin K include blueberries, edamame, soybeans, pumpkin, kale, spinach, collard greens, broccoli, sauerkraut, and pickles. There are many excellent animal sources of vitamin K2, such as fatty meats, liver, dairy foods, and eggs. These foods all provide different nutrients, depending on the animal's diet and where it was sourced.

- **Vitamin B1 (Thiamine)**

The nutrient vitamin B1 is responsible for turning food into energy, and it's found in plant-based foods such as whole-grain cereals, yeast, beans, nuts, and meat can provide vitamin B1 for those not on a strict vegan diet. A lack of B1 can lead to the debilitating disease beriberi, impacting the heart, digestive, and nervous systems.

Did you know that the recommended daily intake of vitamin B1 is different for men and women? For women over 18, the recommended intake is 1.1-1.4 mg, while for men aged 14 and older, the recommended intake is 1.2 mg.

- **Vitamin B6 (Pyridoxine)**

The health benefits of vitamin B6 are vast; it helps keep the immune system functioning properly, aids in normal brain development, and even helps keep our nervous system healthy and in check. This important vitamin is found in many common foods, such as poultry, fish, potatoes, chickpeas, and bananas.

You should aim to consume 1.3 mg of vitamin B6 per day if you are an adult aged 50 or below. However, pregnant or breastfeeding teens and women need up to 2 mg per day to meet their nutritional needs.

- **Vitamin B9 (Folate)**

Folate is essential for maintaining a positive mood. A folate deficiency can lead to depression, so it's important to ensure you're getting enough of this vitamin from your diet. Folate is found in green leafy vegetables, beans, peas, peanuts, other legumes, and citrus fruits.

To ensure you're getting enough folate in your diet, aim for at least 400 mcg daily. This amount is recommended for men and women aged 19 years and older. If you're pregnant or lactating, you'll need 600 mcg and 500 mcg. If you drink alcohol regularly, aim for 600 mcg or more.

- **Vitamin B5 (Pantothenic acid)**

Pantothenic acid is essential for energy production and hormone synthesis in the body. It also helps drive many biochemical reactions in the cells, including the breakdown of carbohydrates and lipids.

You can find vitamin B5 in various foods, including broccoli, kale, avocado, whole-grain cereals, potatoes, dairy, and organ meats. Getting 5 mg of vitamin B5 each day is recommended for all people age 14 and older.

- **Vitamin B3 (Niacin)**

Niacin is essential for energy production in the body. It helps convert food components into usable energy. Good sources of niacin include legumes, nuts, enriched bread, dairy, fish, and lean meats.

You need at least 14 mg of Vitamin B3 each day if you're a girl aged 14 or older; boys in this age group need 16 mg.

- **Vitamin B2 (Riboflavin)**

Riboflavin is a water-soluble vitamin that is essential in the human diet. It helps the body metabolize food into energy and also helps keep the skin, gut, and blood cells healthy. Getting enough riboflavin may help prevent migraine headaches cataracts and boost the immune system. It can also treat acne, muscle cramps, and energy levels.

You can get your daily dose of Vitamin B2 from various natural sources, such as nuts, green vegetables, meat, and dairy products. Did you know that you need only 1.3 mg of vitamin B2 each day if you're a man and 1.1 mg if you're a woman? Pregnant women need 1.4 mg, and breastfeeding mothers should have 1.6 mg.

Tip 8: Drink plenty of water!

They say water is life. I bet most people want to live, so why don't you get some water now! Out of all the common drinks, water is easily the healthiest choice. There are many health benefits from drinking a lot of water. The best way to stay hydrated is to drink at least eight glasses of water per day. So, what are the health benefits of drinking water?

- **Drink water to relieve your constipation**

Water is essential for keeping the body functioning properly, and drinking plenty of it may help prevent and relieve constipation. Mineral water, in particular, can be beneficial for those with constipation as it contains minerals that can help aid digestion.

- **Drink water to prevent your hangovers**

Do you remember the hangovers you experience on Mondays at work after partying all weekend? One way to reduce the symptoms of a hangover is to drink plenty of water. This will help rehydrate the body, which is often a main contributor to the hangover experience.

- **Drink water to have a better skin**

So you want to go to work, you look at yourself through the mirror and see your screen dry! That's enough to make your day horrible. It is common to have dehydration in the wintertime. Dehydration is mostly caused by not drinking enough water. In this case, the skin will become dry, and it will become more susceptible to irritation. So, you should make sure that you drink more water to maintain your skin's hydration as it keeps your skin supple and makes you feel less dry and itchy.

- **Drink water to reduce your risk of formation of kidney stones**

Drinking more water may help decrease your risk of developing kidney stones. This is because taking more fluids increases the volume of urine passing through the kidneys. This dilutes the concentration of minerals, so kidney stones are less likely to crystallize and form clumps.

- **Drink water to reduce your headaches**

Water is essential for optimal health and can help reduce the severity and frequency of headaches. When you drink enough water, you'll feel more energized and alert due to better oxygen circulation throughout your body. More than half of your body weight is composed of water, and dehydration can impair your brain function, causing you to feel tired and experience more headaches. So make sure to drink plenty of water every day to stay healthy and headache-free!

- **Drink water to retain your energy levels throughout the day**

Mild dehydration can harm your energy levels, mood, and memory. Ensuring you drink enough water can help boost your energy and replace any lost electrolytes.

- **Drink enough water if you want to lose weight**

Drinking water before meals can help suppress your appetite, leading to weight loss. Also, drinking water can help reduce your overall liquid calorie intake, contributing to weight loss.

CHAPTER THREE: HOW TO GET STARTED ON A MEDITERRANEAN DIET

The Mediterranean Diet Guide to Help You Start Today: Here's How To Live A Healthier Life Like The Greeks.

The Mediterranean diet is a flavorful and healthy way of eating that is based on the traditional

foods found in countries bordering the Mediterranean Sea. French, Spanish, Greek, and Italian cuisine. The Mediterranean diet emphasizes the consumption of nutrient-rich plant-based foods. These include eating healthy whole grains, fresh fruits, vegetables, nuts, and heart-healthy fats like olive oil. And because fish, seafood, dairy, and poultry are included in moderation, it's a balanced way to eat. Red meat and sweets are eaten only occasionally. The Mediterranean diet has been shown to reduce the risk of heart disease, cancer, diabetes, high blood pressure, osteoporosis, and obesity, as well as the risk of other chronic illnesses like Alzheimer's Parkinson's. The Mediterranean diet is good for every organ in the body. The data also suggests that it helps prevent dementia and improves immune function. The Mediterranean diet is low in fat, which can help control weight.

Oldways' Mediterranean Diet Pyramid and the **USDA's MyPlate** provide helpful guides for eating at every meal.

Mediterranean Diet Pyramid

- The Mediterranean diet pyramid recommends that you base every meal around nutrient-rich vegetables and fruits, especially those that are dark in color, for maximum antioxidant protection! Legumes and beans, whole grains, nuts, and olive oil are also key components of a healthy Mediterranean diet, so be sure to include them in your meals often.
- The Mediterranean diet pyramid also recommends that you eat fish and seafood at least two times a week to get the many health benefits of this type of diet.
- You can enjoy moderate servings of poultry, dairy, cheese, and eggs every day or every week while on a Mediterranean diet. Plus, for red wine (typically with meals), women can have one glass per day, and men can have two glasses per day.
- You can enjoy a delicious and nutritious Mediterranean diet while still indulging in your favorite sweets and red meat occasionally.
- The diet encourages regular physical activity, and 30 minutes a day is recommended. You can also make the diet more enjoyable by incorporating family dinners. And don't forget to drink water!

MyPlate

- The USDA's MyPlate initiative recommends making at least half of your grains in your diet whole grains. Whole grains contain the entire grain kernel, including the bran, germ, and endosperm. Examples of whole grains include whole-wheat flour, bulgur (cracked wheat), oatmeal, whole-grain cornmeal, and brown rice. A food considered a whole grain food is made with 100% whole grains.

- There are many ways to enjoy the fruit - fresh, frozen, canned, or dried/dehydrated - and you can enjoy it whole, cut-up, pureed, or cooked. MyPlate recommends getting at least half of your fruit fix from whole fruit rather than 100% fruit juice.

- There are all sorts of ways to enjoy vegetables - they can be cooked or eaten raw, fresh or frozen, canned or dried. No matter how you choose to eat them, vegetables are a healthy and delicious part of any diet. The USDA's MyPlate recommends that you vary your veggies to get the most benefit from their unique nutrients and health benefits.

- You can mix up your protein routine by choosing different meat, poultry, seafood, and vegetarian options. Lean or low-fat meats, like 93% lean ground beef, pork loin, and skinless chicken breasts, are recommended. Seafood higher in beneficial fatty acids (omega-3s) and lower in methylmercury, such as salmon, anchovies, and trout, is a good choice. Beans, peas, lentils, nuts, seeds, and soy products are great vegetarian protein sources.

- The Dairy Group is a great place to find nutrient-rich foods like milk, yogurt, cheese, fortified soy milk, and yogurt. These foods are packed with important nutrients like calcium and protein, which can help keep you healthy and strong. USDA'S MyPlate recommends moving to low-fat or fat-free dairy milk or yogurt (or lactose-free dairy or fortified soy versions) to get the most out of the Dairy Group.

CHAPTER FOUR: HOW TO GET STARTED ON A WHOLE-FOOD PLANT-BASED LIFESTYLE

The Complete Guide on Getting Started on The Whole Food Plant-Based Lifestyle.

Every so often, I hear my friends say things like "I don't feel like I have time for a whole-food plant-based diet!" or "I'm not that serious about a whole-food plant-based diet, but it would be nice to make one of them part of my lifestyle." Choosing a healthy lifestyle is one of the best things you can do for your body. Today, more and more people opt for the whole food plant-based diet, also known as WFPB. It's simple to follow, nutritious, and best of all, it's easy to stick with it! Whether you're interested in losing weight or keeping well, this should be something you try. This diet will leave you feeling fantastic.

Although sometimes confused with other diet plans, like veganism, the whole food plant-based diet is a far more encompassing program.

The WFPB diet itself is not just a diet, but more of a way of life that focuses on eating mostly plants, including vegetables, fruits, whole grains, legumes, seeds, and nuts, while cutting out heavily processed foods, like highly refined grain products, foods with added sugars or artificial sweeteners and foods with added fat.

Whole food plant-based diets aren't new but are something that many people are reviving to help them achieve their health and wellness goals. The term whole-food plant-based diet became popular towards the end of the 20th century.

Dietitians used the phrase to distinguish it from vegetarian diets, which often relied on processed foods and animal products that were technically still "plant-based." WFPB diets are distinguished because they only include foods that can be obtained through plant sources and exclude all animal products.While it may seem like a complex way to eat, many people have successfully used this diet for chronic conditions such as high blood pressure, diabetes, heart disease, overweight, obesity, cancer, and inflammatory bowel diseases. Research has shown that these diets may also help reverse chronic illness, improve quality of life and reduce medical costs.

How a Whole Food Plant-Based Food Diet May Take Care of Your Health

1. You can lose some weight.

Whole-food, plant-based diets are a powerful tool for shedding excess pounds and keeping them off for good. Studies have shown that they are incredibly effective for weight loss, and they may also help you maintain your weight in the long run because it's made up of lots of fiber-rich foods and excludes consumption of processed foods. In addition, many WFPB diets are rich in fruits and vegetables, which contribute to satiety. Research indicates that individuals eating a vegetarian diet have lower body weights than those who eat meat.

Eating a balanced, whole-food plant-based diet may also help with weight loss for people trying to lose weight through calorie restriction. This has been demonstrated in numerous studies looking at calorie-restricted plant-based diets. All these can help you with the health problems of being overweight and obese.

2. Your risks of developing type 2 diabetes are reduced.

Whole-food plant-based nutrition may be an effective tool in managing and reducing your risk of developing type 2 diabetes.

A systematic review containing more than 200,000 male and female participants found a diet that emphasized healthy plant foods. In contrast, low in animal foods was associated with a reduction of about 34% in the risk of diabetes.

3. You have reduced risks of developing cancer.

Research suggests that following a plant-based diet may reduce your risk of certain types of cancer. The Academy of Nutrition and Dietetics notes that people who eat a plant-based diet may lower their risk of endometrial, breast, lung, prostate, and colorectal cancers. However, a diet high in processed meat has been linked to an increased risk of colorectal cancer. A healthy vegan diet is lower in fat and calories than the typical American diet. A 2013 study published in the "Journal of the Academy of Nutrition and Dietetics."

4. Your risks of developing Alzheimer's disease and cognitive deficits are reduced.

Some studies have suggested that a diet rich in vegetables and fruits may help slow or prevent cognitive decline and Alzheimer's disease in older adults. For this powerful benefit, some of the most popular foods include spinach, chard, kale, tomatoes, and berries. Researchers from Columbia University in New York City suggest that seniors who eat high amounts of vegetables and fruits may have a reduced risk of developing Alzheimer's disease.

5. You protect the environment by going plant-based

A plant-based diet is a great way to help protect the environment. A new report from the U.N. and Intergovernmental Panel on Climate Change (IPCC) says that a global shift to a plant-based diet is vital to avoiding the worst impacts of climate change. The report says animal agriculture is responsible for more greenhouse gas emissions than all the world's transportation systems combined, primarily due to clearing forests for farmland and methane released by livestock.

What to eat in a Whole-Food Plant-Based Diet?

When transitioning to a plant-based diet, aim to center your meals around nutrient-rich plant-based foods. If animal foods are eaten, try to include them in smaller quantities and be mindful of the item's quality.

- **Eat fruits** such as berries, citrus fruits, pears, peaches, pineapple, bananas, stone fruit (including plums, apricots, cherries, and nectarines), melons, apples, grapes, and raisins.
- **Eat starchy vegetables** such as Potatoes, sweet potatoes, butternut squash, celery root, carrots, parsnips, beets, and more. They're rich in fiber and nutrients. Low-carbohydrate vegetables are also excellent sources of fiber, vitamins, and minerals. Try to eat 2 or 3 cups of vegetables every day. It will help you to maintain a healthy body weight. You'll get plenty of fiber and antioxidants. If possible, choose organic vegetables since they are free from pesticides and other chemicals.
- **Eat non-starchy vegetables** such as broccoli, kale, cauliflower, spinach, peppers, tomatoes, carrots, asparagus, etc.
- **Whole grains** such as brown rice, brown rice pasta, quinoa, rolled oats, barley and farro are excellent options.
- **Healthy fats** such as avocados, olive oil, and unsweetened coconut can be taken on a Whole-food plant-based diet (WFPB).
- **Legumes** such as Peas, chickpeas, lentils, peanuts, black beans can be taken on a Whole-food plant-based diet.
- **Seeds** such as Sunflower seeds, sesame seeds, and flaxseed can be taken on a Whole-food plant-based diet. These foods are a good source of vitamins, minerals, fiber, and essential fatty acids.

- **Consider taking nuts** such as macadamia cashews.
- **Take unsweetened plant-based milk** such as cashew milk, coconut milk, and almond milk.
- **Spices, herbs,** such as salt, turmeric, basil, black pepper, rosemary, curry.
- **Seasonings** such as salsa, mustard, and nutritional yeast can also be added to your diet: vinegar, lemon, lime juice, and other condiments.

- **You can also add plant protein** such as tofu or tempeh. Plant protein from sources or powders with no added sugars or artificial ingredients can also help.
- **Don't forget to include beverages** such as tea, coffee, tea, sparkling water.

If you're looking to add some animal products to your plant-based diet, make sure to buy high-quality groceries from your local store, or better yet, get them from a local farm:

- Locally grown food can be purchased at a farmers market, community-supported agriculture (CSA), or other local sources.
- Buy organic whenever possible
- GMOs should be limited in consumption
- It would be best if you only bought 100% grass-fed meats
- Source eggs and poultry raised in pasture

Limit these foods when you're on a Whole-food plant-based diet.

When following a WFPB diet, aim to avoid highly processed foods and minimize your intake of animal products. These foods include:

- Fast food includes French fries, cheeseburgers, hot dogs, and chicken nuggets. Sweets and added sugars such as soda, sweet tea, table sugar, juice, pastries, cookies, candy, sugary cereals, and so on.
- White rice, white pasta, white bread, bagels, and other refined grains
- Packaged and ready-to-eat foods include chips, crackers, cereal bars, frozen dinners, and so on.
- Vegan-friendly processed foods include plant-based meats such as Tofurkey, faux cheeses, vegan butter, and so on.
- Equal, Splenda, Sweet'N Low, and other artificial sweeteners
- Bacon, lunch meats, sausage, beef jerky, and other processed animal products.

CHAPTER FIVE: HOW TO GET STARTED ON A FLEXITARIAN DIET

Here's How You Can Reap The Benefits of Plant-Based Foods While Enjoying Your Meat In Moderation.

This diet, created by Dawn Jackson Blatner, enables people to reap the benefits of vegetarian eating while enjoying animal products in moderation. It is also known as the Semi-vegetarian diet. People following this diet are primarily vegetarian, consuming lots of fruits, vegetables, whole grains, beans, nuts, seeds, and legumes, including a small amount of meat, poultry, fish, and seafood. They might include dairy foods and eggs, depending on personal preference. This flexible type of eating is an excellent starting point that will allow you more flexibility when it comes time to start incorporating plant-based meals into your everyday life!

The "Flexitarian" way of life has no clear-cut rules as to how many calories or grams of protein, fat, and carbohydrates can be eaten in a day. It's not even really a diet in the traditional sense. It's more of a lifestyle choice because they choose to "veg out" at least once or twice a week by leaving animal flesh uneaten on their plate.

Vegetarians thrive on Flexitarianism because they still get their recommended amount of animal products each day without going whole-hog into the carnivorous territory.

Does a Flexitarian Diet have health benefits?

With so many people interested in plant-based diets, the Flexitarian Diet has become a natural choice for many who are curious about vegetarianism and like the idea of eating meat when they want to. But this diet is also an excellent choice for anyone looking to improve their health or anyone who doesn't have the energy to give up meat entirely.

The Flexitarian Diet focuses on the health benefits of eating plants and emphasizes the importance of getting these foods with every meal. So, what are the benefits of this type of diet?

1. Your risk of developing Type 2 diabetes is reduced.

A study in over 60,000 participants found that the prevalence of type 2 diabetes was 1.5% lower in flexitarians compared to non-vegetarians. This is most likely because plant-based diets such as the Flexitarian Diet may aid in weight loss, and they also contain many foods high in fiber and low in unhealthy fats and added sugar. Eating a healthy diet, especially a predominantly plant-based one, may help prevent and manage this disease.

2. A Flexitarian Diet can help you lose weight.

If you're trying intuitive eating, there are some seemingly endless eating plans and diets to choose from, but flexitarianism is one of the more credible ones. Suppose you emphasize the plant-based component in this lifestyle by utilizing vegetarian recipes (that also happen to be low fat). In that case, you'll almost certainly feel full with fewer calories than before, which is what makes shedding pounds almost inevitable! A review of studies in more than 1,100 people was completed at Texas Tech University, and it found that those who went on a vegetarian diet for 18 weeks lost an average of 4.5 pounds (2 kilograms) more than those who weren't practicing this eating plan due to their high fiber content and less saturated fats.

3. Your risk of developing heart disease is reduced.

If you've been thinking about eating a vegetarian diet or are already in the midst of a healthy vegetarian eating plan, you'll be glad to know that keeping your heart healthy is one more reason to keep on with it! A new study recently found that adults who follow vegetarian diets have a 32% lower risk of suffering from coronary heart disease. Relying on a range of veggies and high-fiber foods, and eating plenty of plant-based protein like beans and nuts, could help reduce blood pressure levels.

4. Your cancer risk is significantly reduced.

Did you know that fruits, vegetables, nuts, seeds, whole grains, and legumes all have antioxidants that may help reduce your cancer risk? Research suggests that vegetarian diets tend to be associated with a lower overall incidence of all cancers. A 7-year study found that semi-vegetarians were 8% less likely to get a particular type of cancer than non-vegetarians! Switching to more vegetarian foods, for instance, eating flexitarian style, could reduce your cancer risk.

5. Switching to the Flexitarian Diet is good for the environment.

Highlighting research about plant-based lifestyles and our impact on the environment could help change perceptions, allowing us to turn more people into Flexitarians! A study found that if those with a Western diet reduced their meat consumption by 10% while increasing consumption of fruits and veggies to fill the gaps, currently cultivated cropland could be decreased by 3.1 million km^2— equivalent to a forest larger than the US state of Oregon! It's crucial as an entrepreneur working in the food market that you keep up with trends to best inform your audience about how they may benefit others and the planet when switching over to a Flexitarian Diet.

There are especially some precautions people take when replacing their usual diet with a plant-based one, and it's pretty easy to see why.

Because while they can boast the benefits mentioned before - lowering cholesterol, reducing your risk of contracting heart disease, obesity, and other diseases that come as a consequence of eating meat, it's important to mention that for most people, this kind of diet has significant drawbacks. For example, it does not contain Vitamin B12 or vitamin D typically found in animal flesh or eggs.

Studies have shown that Vitamin B12 deficiency is prevalent among vegetarians, specifically pregnant vegetarian mothers and older people who avoid animal products. While one's diet does not include any animal products according to the dictionary definition, anyone living off of protein supplements like meat purchases can be considered a flexitarian. Although eating a flexitarian diet may seem convenient on the surface, many people don't realize that they are at risk for developing a Vitamin B12 deficiency just as vegetarians are. This could lead to dangerous health issues over time, which is why everyone, including irregular consumers, should make sure that they get enough B vitamins in their daily diets.

Vegetarians can have difficulty physically enduring throughout the day due to a lack of physical endurance since they are not getting all the needed proteins in their diet. There are also some good stores of zinc and iron that one needs to supplement, as these minerals are best absorbed from animal foods. Suppose a person likes leafy green vegetables and beans. In that case, they will probably be able to maintain healthy levels of Vitamin C, which increases how much iron one absorbs into the body. They may want to eat seeds and nuts on this diet to get adequate zinc. Also, nuts and seeds that do not have an outer shell can be harder to digest than fried ones with shells intact would be to chew through first.

Flexitarians should be wary of getting enough omega-3 fatty acids in their diet, typically one of the most challenging things to get right. However, there are ways you can incorporate ALA into your diet through these great sources: Walnuts, chia seeds, and flaxseeds.

Foods that you should eat when on a Flexitarian diet

1. Plant proteins

You don't have to throw in the towel when eating healthy while following a Flexitarian diet! There are several plant proteins out there you can use without feeling like you're sacrificing the dishes you grew up loving so much. Try out some substitutes like peas or lentils like black beans, pinto beans, garbanzo beans, white beans, red lentils, soybeans, tofu, tempeh, legumes, and lentils!

2. Non-starchy vegetables

The Flexitarian Diet encourages you to try and eat predominantly non-starchy vegetables as they may offer you some of the most benefits. Try to eat greens, bell peppers, Brussels sprouts, and other green beans. And make sure not to forget the carrot cauliflower.

3. Starchy vegetables

When it comes to being a Flexitarian, you will want to aim to eat a diet rich in starches by enjoying Winter squash and other kinds of squashes, peas, sweet potatoes, and corn.

4. Whole grains

It's easy being a Flexitarian. Just eat whole grains that include quinoa, brown rice, oats, barley, sorghum, buckwheat, teff, and farro! Promote Meatless Mondays!

5. Nuts and seeds

Give yourself a high five! On this diet, you're going to be adding more to your plate than just colorful veggies. You should try to eat nuts and seeds such as almonds, flaxseeds, chia seeds, walnuts, cashews, and pistachios. They are rich in protein and essential minerals such as zinc, iron, and potassium. They are also rich in healthy fats.

6. Fruits

A Flexitarian diet is all about tasting the very best of fruits, so you do have to leave room for some imperfection. Eat fruits such as grapes, apples, cherries, oranges, and berries.

7. Plant-based milk alternatives

Nowadays, eating healthy is a top priority for many people. And while you may desire to eat healthier and give your body everything it needs, you might also crave comfort food or feel lazy at times. It's not easy. When this happens, the best thing to do is to replace unhealthy meals with something else that's better for us. This can be as simple as an alternative source of protein or simply switching from butter to olive oil! On a Flexitarian diet, you can try plant-based milk alternatives such as soy milk, coconut, unsweetened almond, and hemp.

8. Condiments

If you're thinking about jumping in with both feet and joining the Flexitarian lifestyle, make sure to use condiments sparingly to keep calories down. Consume things like rice vinegar, salsa, mustard, nutritional yeast, and ketchup without added sugar.

9. Herbs, Seasonings, Spices

Herbs and spices are good for you. These foods can help reduce feelings of fatness but be careful about the number of seasonings you use in your cooking because additives may not agree with you. With a Flexitarian diet, include Herbs, spices, and seasonings that are healthy choices, including Basil, Oregano, Mint, Thyme, and Turmeric.

10. Beverages

It's essential to have a balanced diet. Since a Flexitarian diet permits the eating of both vegetables, fruits, grains, and meats, it's a way for individuals who do not need to reduce calories too much to be still able to control the kind of calories they are consuming. The key is moderation in everything, including how you drink your beverages. Some great options for drinks on this diet include water, black tea or green tea, unsweetened coffee, and sparkling water. But remember that anything you consume, even in moderation, may pile up into unwanted weight, so always keep track of how much you're drinking just as much as you might be tracking what foods go over what amounts of carbs or sugar, etc. to help make sure your body is always functioning at its best.

When following a Flexitarian diet, be sure that you choose eggs that come from hens that have been allowed to roam freely around their chicken run, fish caught wild rather than farmed, and grass-fed meat and dairy products (you do not want the animals raised on grains because it is not in their natural diet). They taste great! In summary:

- Buy locally grown food can be purchased at a farmers market, community-supported agriculture (CSA), or other local sources.
- Buy organic whenever possible.
- GMOs should be limited in consumption.

- You should only buy 100% grass-fed meats
- Source eggs and poultry raised in pasture

CHAPTER SIX: HOW TO GET STARTED ON A VEGETARIAN DIET

Do You Want To Enjoy Your Favorite Animal Foods In Moderation? Try a Vegetarian diet

Vegetarians can consume more fruits, vegetables, whole grains, and calcium-rich foods. With a bit of forward-thinking, you will be able to meet your family's needs without too much hassle with some easy-to-understand tips. Vegetarianism continues to grow in popularity for a myriad of reasons. Overall good health is usually one reason people choose a vegetarian diet, this means not only are you reducing your risk of certain diseases and illnesses, but you're also adding more lean proteins into your diet and upping your fiber while lowering fat and cholesterol intake! Unlike meat-based products, though, many vegetarian foods are processed, which can create problems regarding appropriate nutritional intake.

There are different types of vegetarian diets:

- **Pescatarian**: Someone who eats fish and seafood, dairy, eggs, and honey but eliminates all meat and poultry from their diet.
- **Lacto-Ovo Vegetarian**: Someone who eats dairy, eggs, and honey but eliminates all animal flesh (meat, poultry, fish, seafood).

- **Lacto-vegetarian**: Eats dairy and honey but eliminates all other animal products.
- **Ovo-vegetarian**: Eat eggs and honey but eliminate all other animal products.
- **Vegan**: Eliminates all animal products, including honey.

The Health Benefits of a Vegetarian Diet

1. Your risk of developing Type 2 diabetes is reduced.

The first step to curbing your blood sugar levels is to change what you're eating. A vegetarian diet, which focuses on grains and nutrient-rich vegetables and fruits, may help you keep your blood sugar stable. Several studies suggest that vegetarians might be less likely to develop type 2 diabetes or to see a relapse after diagnosis. For example, one extensive review of six fundamental studies showed that people who switched from a non-vegetarian diet to a vegetarian (or semi-vegetarian) diet had a 53% lower risk of developing type 2 diabetes in the next five years. The same kind of eating change also appeared to reduce their chances for relapse if they already had type 2 diabetes.

2. You stand a better chance of losing weight when you go the vegetarian lifestyle.

Swapping to a vegetarian diet can be an effective strategy if you want to lose weight. One study of 120 participants over 24 weeks has shown that veggie people weighed on average 4.5 fewer pounds (2 kg) than non-vegetarians! Even though this was only a small-scale study with limited participants and should probably not be taken at face value - it's still pretty promising news for those with meat-free ambitions, whether it's for their health or animal rights reasons!

3. Vegetarian Diets are healthy for your heart.

Vegetarian diets are heart-healthy. Several studies demonstrate that a vegetarian diet will help keep your heart strong and healthy. In one study, researchers looked at 76 participants who followed a vegetarian diet for an average of 4 years. The researchers found reduced triglyceride, total cholesterol, and "bad" LDL cholesterol levels in all participants who followed a vegan, lacto-vegetarian, or ovo-vegetarian diet compared to those in this group who ate meat occasionally or regularly. Several other studies have also demonstrated reduced blood pressure levels and better health in those following plant-based diets.

If you're interested in lowering your risk for heart disease or simply increasing the odds of avoiding a life-threatening condition that can lead to death if undiagnosed and not treated properly, then it's definitely worth giving a vegetarian diet a try!

4. You stand a better chance against cancer risk when you go Vegetarian.

Some more recent research shows that a vegetarian diet helps decrease your chances of getting cancer. However, it seems that not all groups benefit from this same treatment. The American Dietetic Association suggests that vegetarians experience fewer colon and gastrointestinal cancers than those who eat meat. They also even suggest going as far as to say that this could be due to "the exclusion of meat and resultant lowering or elimination of consumption of animal fat." Additionally, the ADA suggests limiting consumption of fat-free meats, such as hot dogs and sausage, because they are high in sodium nitrates which might raise blood pressure.

The Cons of a Vegetarian Diet.

So you're a vegetarian, huh? Well, that's great! For the most part, being a vegetarian is a healthy choice. It has been shown to reduce your risk of cardiovascular disease, boost your life expectancy and slow down heart disease. A balanced vegetarian diet can be healthful, but it may also lead to nutritional deficiencies. So what are the deficiencies associated with this diet?

Meat, poultry, and fish are excellent sources of protein and omega-3 fatty acids, as well as micronutrients like zinc, selenium, vitamins E and B12. Other animal products like dairy tend to be abundant in calcium, vitamin D, and the above essential vitamins. If you cut these foods from your diet, it is recommended that you get them from other sources.

It's well known that vegetarians are prone to becoming deficient in certain vital nutrients. For example, they're more likely to suffer from calcium, iron, iodine, and vitamin B12 deficiencies than the average person - these essential micronutrients are vital to sustaining life and play critical roles in many body processes, including energy production. One of the most common deficiency symptoms is fatigue, leading to weakness, anemia, and bone loss if slighted for too long. Thinning hair or hair loss can also occur due to a lack of iodine in the diet! Just ensure you're getting enough vitamins by including various fruits and vegetables in your diet at least twice a day, as well as protein sources like beans, nuts, foods, and milk. You might consider fortified foods - they're great ways to get lots of extra vitamins into drink form!

Don't forget that multivitamins or supplements may be able to fill any gaps in your diet quickly, so it may be worth considering.

Foods to Eat on a Vegetarian Diet.

A healthy vegetarian diet includes a range of quality eats - plenty of greens and other healthy veggies, grains, good fats, and some protein-packed choices like beans and seeds. If you have a Lacto-Ovo vegetarian diet plan, milk products can also contribute to your daily protein intake. If you're vegan, remember that this diet is the most restrictive form of vegetarianism, which bans meat and any animal-source food, including poultry, fish, eggs, and dairy products. So check out these awesome foods that you should start eating now!

- **Grab Those Fruits**

Fruit salads are great, so why not have one for breakfast today? A few healthy fruits to eat on a vegetarian diet are oranges, apples, pears, bananas, berries, melons, and peaches!

- **Eat Nuts**

When you're a vegetarian, nuts are a must. "Go Nuts for Vegetarian Nuts – including almonds, cashews, walnuts and more."

- **Eat lots of Vegetables**.

When you're on a vegetarian diet, try to include vegetables such as spinach, green beans, broccoli, brussels sprouts, and tomatoes. And don't forget your carrots!

- **Get your proteins now!**

When you're on a vegetarian diet, filling your plate with proteins such as tempeh, tofu, seitan, and nutritional yeast is just one way to make sure you're getting enough nutrients and trace minerals for sustained energy throughout the day. However, when eating out, it can be tricky, if not impossible, to point out which dishes might not yet contain eggs or dairy products for those who are vegan. When in restaurants, I recommend that you always inform the waiter of your dietary preferences so they can double-check with the chefs to avoid any mix-ups.

- **Eat Seeds**

Eat flax, chia, and hemp to get your seeds when you're on a vegetarian diet! Flax seeds, chia seeds, and hemp seeds are some of the best natural sources for individuals who eat a vegetarian diet. Among other health benefits, these foods contain heart-healthy Omega 3 fatty acids. Some studies have suggested that by eating them regularly, one may reduce their risk of developing heart diseases like arteries clogging, leading to stroke caused by blockages in blood flow and high cholesterol, leading to oxidative stress damage throughout the body.

If you want to start eating healthier and leaner while also satisfying your taste buds - these are the kinds of foods to reach for next time you're at the store.

- **Eat Legumes**

If you're trying to go vegetarian and looking to get healthy, make sure you incorporate legumes into your diet every day. Using them in place of other animal sources can help boost protein intake and keep one feeling full and satisfied for long periods. Eat legumes such as lentils, beans, and peas. Chickpeas are also fine to eat.

- **Eat healthy fats**

When following a vegetarian diet, it is essential to ingest healthy fats to keep you energized, such as olive oil and avocado.

- **Eat Grains**

Some vegetarian ingredients will help you make the most out of your healthy lifestyle. Make sure you incorporate grains into your menus, such as quinoa, barley, buckwheat, and rice, to ensure your body gets all the nutrients it needs!

Foods That Should Avoid In a Vegetarian Diet.

You might be required to alter your diet as a vegetarian. Lacto-Ovo vegetarianism, the most common form, has adherents that exclude meat, poultry, and fish. Other types may abstain from foods like eggs or dairy products. A vegan diet is the strictest form of vegetarianism because it excludes all plant foods from animals, such as eggs or dairy products.

The best type of diet for you depends on your body and dietary preferences! All in all, you might need to avoid the following foods when on a vegetarian diet.

- **Avoid Eggs**

If you're a vegan or vegetarian, eggs are something that you should avoid.

- **Avoid Meat**

Some excellent reasons to avoid eating meat include an overall healthy and lighter diet. For some, avoiding meat also helps animals and the world. If you're in the mood for a meal that's vegetarian, there is a large variety of foods you can find to try. These are all good options to get your nutrients.

- **Avoid Meat-based ingredients**

Being a vegetarian can be difficult when making meals, especially if one does not know any specific ingredients to stay away from. Some ingredients to avoid for the vegetarian diet include gelatin, lard, carmine, isinglass, oleic acid, and suet.

- **Avoid Dairy Products**

Dairy products are only found in animals' milk, such as yogurt and cheese. For vegans and ovo-vegetarians, they don't consume dairy even if they use it while cooking.

- **Avoid Fish**

It's essential to be wary of which fish types you consume, and when it comes to this diet, you also need to pay close attention to which seafood you're eating. It's recommended that vegetarians pay some extra special consideration to these types of seafood: bass, catfish, cod, crab, crayfish, eel, halibut, lobster, monkfish, mussels, scallops, and shrimp. Restrictions on eating fish should not apply to Pescetarians.

- **Avoid Poultry**

Some people should avoid eating poultry like chicken and turkey when on a vegetarian diet.

- **Avoid Honey**

Vegetarians who practice veganism may choose to avoid honey, beeswax, and pollen.

CHAPTER SEVEN: HOW TO GET STARTED ON A VEGAN DIET

Complete Guide to Starting a Vegan Diet. Should You Go For This Restrictive Vegetarian Diet?

Vegans are followers of a lifestyle who try their best not to consume anything or do anything  that would otherwise cause harm or pain to an animal. This means not eating any meat and neither wearing any fur or leather. The vegan diet is nearly the opposite of what most people follow daily, meaning vegans won't have bacon for breakfast, steak for lunch, and chicken for dinner; instead, fruit, vegetables, grains, and legumes in addition to soybean products.

Types of Dietary Vegans

1. Raw Vegan Diet

Raw vegans eat a large majority of uncooked or heated food at temperatures below 48°C (118°F). They get the majority of their nutrients from consuming fresh fruits, vegetables, nuts, seeds, and legumes sprouted.

2. Whole-food vegan diet

A whole-food vegan diet is one of the most healthful ways to eat, according to Dr. Michael Greger and Dr. T. Colin Campbell. It's characterized by the consumption of a wide variety of unprocessed and whole plant foods such as fruits, vegetables, whole grains, legumes, and a few nuts or seeds here and there.

3. High-carb-low-fat vegan (HCLF) diet

A high-carb-low, fat vegan diet is all the rage these days, with many celebs jumping on board and making it a part of their daily lives. The great thing about HCLF is that you can shed weight without the fryings, blanching, and sautéing of veggies, as is typically required with a low-fat diet. Not to mention that they taste great, even when baked! That being said, avoiding oils will emit fewer greenhouse gases in your home and fewer toxins in your body.

 Another plus? You'll be able to save money because you won't have to keep buying vegetable oil at the supermarket anymore!

4. Junk-food vegan diet

The junk-food vegan diet is a type of vegan diet lacking in whole plant foods. These diets rely heavily on mock meats and cheese, fries, vegan desserts, and other heavily processed foods, which include extremely high levels of fat and salt.

Why should you go the Vegan way?

- **You stand a better chance of losing weight when you go Vegan.**

Vegan diets have proven to be very good for weight loss. One of the main reasons is that Vegan diets tend to be naturally lower in calories, which certainly helps overweight or obese individuals reduce their calorie intake in a non-restrictive way. As a result, they naturally lose weight without making any conscious effort, resulting in a higher metabolism rate and body mass index (BMI). Vegan diets have been studied and compared directly to non-vegan diets as part of randomized controlled trials, which set them apart from other diet systems because it takes away the external factors associated with subjects not sticking with their diets.

The results show that vegan dieters' metabolic rates increased by 32%, and those on a vegan diet lost an average of 10 pounds. In contrast, similar trials showed that control groups' eating stayed the same or even gained weight!

- **Your Blood Sugar and risk of developing Type 2 diabetes is better managed by going vegan.**

A vegan diet has been proven to lower blood sugar levels, contribute to higher insulin sensitivity, and help make overweight vegans 78% less likely to fall victim to type 2 diabetes than those who consume high amounts of meat. A big part of this is probably due to the higher fiber intake, which helps slow down the digestion process by making you feel full quicker while simultaneously clearing out your system.

- **Your Heart could be healthier if you go Vegan.**

Observational studies tell us that vegans may have up to a 75% lower risk of developing high blood pressure and a 42% lower risk of dying from heart disease. Several reports show that vegan diets are much more effective than the average diet at reducing blood sugar, LDL, and total cholesterol levels. These effects are especially beneficial since reducing blood pressure, cholesterol, and blood sugar levels reportedly could reduce heart disease risks by up to 46%.

- **Your Cancer risk is reduced when you go Vegan.**

Vegans may benefit from a 15% lower risk of developing or dying from cancer. One reason is that plant-based diets are usually lower in saturated fat and higher in antioxidants, fiber, and phytochemicals like flavonoids, which combat cancer.

- **Arthritis symptoms are better managed by going Vegan**

Vegan diets significantly reduce symptoms of arthritis such as pain, joint swelling, and morning stiffness.

- **Your risk of poor Kidney function is reduced when you go Vegan**

According to some studies, people with diabetes who opt for vegetable proteins instead of meat may benefit from lower rates of decreased function in their kidneys.

- **Go Vegan to save the animals!**

Although you may be small, every individual makes a difference, which is true when going vegan. It doesn't seem like one person can accomplish something big. Still, through dedication, positivity, and support of others during their journey to the same end goal - which is to help animals treated poorly - veganism contributes considerably to making animals happier creatures in an unforgiving world. It all starts with one person!

- **You can go Vegan to save the environment.**

If your diet is largely plant-based, you have the power to reduce carbon dioxide, a major contributor to climate change. Animal agriculture uses more water than producing plant foods and generates a lot of greenhouse gases. Environmentally speaking, going Vegan is a very practical decision to make.

Some Foods That You Should Avoid on a Vegan Diet

When starting on a vegan diet, be sure to plan things out beforehand. Otherwise, you might get overwhelmed with how much more restrictive it is than other forms of vegetarianism that allow meat and fish in moderation. Here are some foods that you need to avoid on a Vegan Diet:

- **Avoid Meat**

Going vegan? Never eat any meat, including beef, pork, or lamb. You should also avoid horse meat as it falls under that category, along with veal, organ meat, and wild game.

- **Avoid Poultry**

When you're on a vegan diet, it's always handy to avoid poultry such as turkey, chicken, goose, or even quails. So instead of consuming poultry, it's healthier to opt for more plant-based proteins such as nuts and seeds. Veganism is a lifestyle choice made possible because of our ever-growing knowledge about environmentally friendly nutrition and eating habits.

- **Avoid Dairy and Dairy Products**

If you're seeking a healthy, vegan lifestyle, it's important to avoid all forms of dairy. This includes milk, butter, yogurt, cheese, and frozen treats like ice cream - however tempting they are!

- **Avoid Fish and other Seafood**

When following a vegan diet, it's important to avoid all types of seafood - especially those that may surprise you! These include octopus, prawns, dorado (Mahi Mahi), squid, etc. Fish is not considered part of the vegan diet and therefore needs to be excluded.

- **Avoid Eggs**

If you're following a vegan diet, please avoid any egg-like products such as those produced by chickens, quails, ostriches, etc., fish and sea mammals.

- **Avoid Honey**

Sometimes it can be difficult to stick to a vegan diet without feeling as if you are missing out on anything because, let's face it, honey is delicious! But vegan folk know that many alternative forms of sweeteners will satisfy your sweet tooth just as well (such as xylitol) and that you get over the initial cravings quickly.

- **Avoid Animal-based ingredients**

While following a vegan diet, be careful about the ingredients you consume. For example: Avoid ' animal sources ' such as Whey, casein, lactose, egg white albumen, and gelatin. On top of that, always check whether vitamin D3 is sourced from an animal source.

Here Are Some Shopping Tips For You

As a vegan, shopping can be tedious because while companies do their best to make all of the foods they produce acceptable for vegans, it's often difficult not to accidentally buy something that you shouldn't eat while at the supermarket or your local grocery stores. When shopping for your favorite vegan foods – remember to always check product labels to make sure that there are no ingredients associated with dairy derived products! Ingredients like whey, casein and lactose may be found in bouillon powder, stock cubes, ketchup and baking mixes available in supermarkets today!

As vegans, we understand that you have limited options when it comes to making the transition from your favorite pudding to the vegan alternative. Lucky for you, there are a few more ingredients out there than just what is listed on this paper. There are two basic ingredients in particular – agar-agar and vege-gel – made from seaweed. These ingredients work effectively in helping to keep the gel or solid state of your favorite desserts as well as helping them maintain their shape once cooled.

As a vegan, you should be sure to always check the labeling of whatever your food products are – dessert or otherwise. The word "vegan" on a product's packaging doesn't necessarily mean that it is absolutely 100% vegan. That's why it's important to carefully read the label in order to make sure there aren't any offending ingredients that may get in the way of your lifestyle.

A good rule of thumb is to remember that anything ending with 'ose' (for example, mevose) denotes non-dairy sugars and should be avoided just as much as common allergens like egg and dairy proteins. When in doubt, steer clear and opt for fortified plant-based dairy alternatives instead!

CHAPTER EIGHT: EASY PLANT-BASED RECIPES

• Grain bowls recipe with lentils and chickpeas

Prep time: 20 minutes

Serving Size: 1 dinner bowl, 4 Serves

Calories: 614

Ingredients

- Lentils. I used 2 cups of cooked brown lentils, drained and rinsed. You can also use canned lentils.
- Extra virgin olive oil. I used Private Reserve Greek EVOO in this recipe. You can also use Early Harvest Extra Virgin Olive Oil or any other brand of your choice.
- Zucchini squash. I used one sliced zucchini
- Farro. I used 2-3 cups (cooked)
- Shallots. I used two sliced shallots
- Parsley. I used 1 cup of fresh parsley (chopped)
- Salt
- Avocados. I used two pitted and sliced avocados.
- Chickpeas. I used 2 cups of cooked chickpeas, drained and rinsed. You can also use canned chickpeas.
- Pitted kalamata olives. I used a handful of kalamata olives
- Cherry tomatoes. I used 2 cups (halved)

Ingredients For the Dressing

- Extra Virgin Olive Oil. I used ⅓ cup
- Fresh lemon juice. I used 2 ½ tablespoons
- Garlic clove. I used one clove, minced
- Mustard. I used 2 ½ teaspoons of Dijon mustard.
- Salt and pepper
- Za'atar spice. I used one teaspoon

- Ground Sumac. I used ½ teaspoon

Directions

1. Heat 2 tablespoons of olive oil over medium-high heat in a frying pan and saute the sliced zucchini until it's slightly tender. To brown it more, lower the temperature to medium.

Notes

Here's How to cook lentils

If you'd rather use dried lentils, these are the steps. First, rinse a bunch of lentils in cold water. Then throw 1 cup of lentils in a pot along with 2.5 cups of water. Bring to a boil and then simmer for 20 minutes or until tender with a pinch of salt added in at the end, and that's all it takes!

- ## Roasted White Beans with Vegetable

Prep Time: 10 minutes

Cook Time: 1 hour 30 minutes

Servings: 2

Ingredients

- 1¼ cup dry white beans
- ½ cup olive oil
- One red bell pepper chopped into small pieces
- One green bell pepper chopped into small pieces
- One onion grated
- One garlic clove sliced
- 7-8 cherry tomatoes halved
- One tablespoon oregano
- One teaspoon tomato paste diluted with 1/4 cup of water

- Ground Pepper
- Salt to taste

Description

1. Soak beans overnight. Rinse, cover and simmer your beans for 30 minutes until soft, and drain them before setting them aside.
2. Preheat your oven to 180 C
3. Chop the veggies and mix peppers, grated onion, garlic, beans, olive oil, tomato paste mixture, oregano, and pepper in a large bowl. Gently mix to incorporate each ingredient.
4. Add the halved cherry tomatoes to your mix of ingredients and mix gently until their color has blended in.
5. Pour your mixed ingredients into a casserole dish
6. Remove zucchini from heat using a slotted spoon and place on paper towels to drain excess oil, then season lightly with salt.
7. Pour all of the dressing ingredients in a glass jar, be sure not to forget any, then close the lid tightly and give it a good shake. Set aside for now but give it another good shake before using.
8. Take four dinner bowls and pour the cooked farro and lentils equally. Each bowl should have about ½ cup of each. Add the cooked zucchini, chopped tomatoes, shallots, and avocado slices to the bowls. Using a teaspoon, sprinkle parsley on top with kalamata olives. Next season lightly with salt, za'atar, and pepper to taste. Add crumbled feta to top if desired just before serving.
9. Feel free to serve at room temperature or warm if farro and pulses were just cooked. Toss ingredients in each bowl and make sure everything is properly incorporated to allow for optimal flavor. If you have any dressing leftover, serve alongside.
10. Add ¼ cup hot water to your casserole dish, and pour in a corner tilting the dish so that the water spreads. You do not want to pour over the olive oil; otherwise, it will get washed off.
11. Place foil on the dish and roast for about 1 hour until peppers become soft. Remove foil and crisp up for about 10 minutes if you prefer a little bit of browning.

12. Switch off your oven, open the door and take out your food. Set your roasted White Beans with Vegetables aside to cool, and then season them with salt if you decide that it needs it.

13. You're free to serve plain or with some feta cheese.

- **Falafel**

Ingredients

- Dried chickpeas
- Fresh herbs
- Onion
- Garlic
- Kosher salt and pepper
- Spices
- Baking powder
- Sesame seeds

Description

1. Soak some chickpeas overnight. Please put them in a bowl, cover with plenty of water and add ½ teaspoon of baking soda. By the end of it, they should look at least twice their original size. Drain them very well.

2. Place chickpeas, onion, spices, fresh herbs (parsley, cilantro, and dill), garlic, and into a food processor, and pulse until the mixture begins to resemble a coarse meal.

3. Put the falafel mix in a bowl and leave it in the fridge for at least an hour or overnight. It will help hold things together better so that the patties will be more easily formed.

4. Stir the chilled mixture into the baking powder and add sesame seeds. Scoop the mixture into golf ball-sized balls, then form into balls or even patties if that's how you'd like to roll (do not flatten them down too far, though, as you want your patties to be friendly and fluffy when ready to cook)

5. Heat the oil until it looks like it bubbles. Ensure your oil is hot enough (around 350-375 degrees F) but not too hot, or the falafel will fall apart.

6.   Don't put in too many falafels at once, or else your frier will be packed for a long time, making you wait for your order. Fry the falafel for about 3-5 minutes until medium brown.

• **Creamy Greek salad pasta**

Prep Time: 20 min

Cook Time: 12 min

Servings: 4-5

Calories: 663 kcal

Ingredients

- 1 pound fusilli pasta, you can also use penne, rigatoni, farfalle or elbow macaroni pasta
- Two large tomatoes, diced
- Two small Persian cucumbers, diced (or about 1 cup chopped English cucumber).
- 1/2 red onion, finely chopped
- 1/2 red bell pepper, chopped
- 1/2 cup sliced olives
- 7 oz (200 grams) feta cheese, cubed or crumbled
- 1 cup corn kernels (I buy them frozen and cook them in boiling water for 2 minutes)
- 1 cup strained Greek yogurt 2% fat (you can also use full fat)
- 1/2 cup parsley, chopped
- 1-2 teaspoons dried oregano
- 2-3 tablespoons extra virgin olive oil
- Salt and pepper to taste

Description

1. Cut all the veggies about the same size
2. Use the instructions on the package to cook pasta and drain it using a colander. Rinse the pasta with cold water until it's no longer warm. Set it aside to drain.

3. In a large bowl, add all of your ingredients and mix gently until everything is combined. Taste and adjust salt.

4. You can serve it immediately or place it in the refrigerator for 1 hour to chill.

• Vibrant Orange & Arugula Salad

Prep Time: 15 minutes

Cook Time: 5 minutes

Servings: 6

Ingredients

For The Salad

- ¼ cup sliced almonds
- 5 to 6 ounces baby arugula
- Two oranges, peeled and cut into thin rounds
- 2 ounces goat cheese, crumbled (about ½ cup)
- ¼ cup thinly sliced and roughly chopped radishes
- Pinch of ground cinnamon, to sprinkle on top

For The Lemon dressing

- ¼ cup extra-virgin olive oil
- Three tablespoons lemon juice
- 1 ½ teaspoon honey
- ¼ teaspoon salt

Description

1. Put a skillet over medium heat and warm the almonds until they are fragrant and just starting to turn golden on the edges. Stir frequently so that you don't burn them (don't worry about too much stirring – you want them to be brown but not burn!). Transfer them to a bowl to cool, about 5 minutes.

2. Place the arugula in a large serving bowl. Add the toasted almonds, chopped oranges, goat cheese, and radishes and lightly sprinkle with a pinch of cinnamon. Set aside until needed.

3. In a small bowl, combine the ingredients: olive oil, lemon juice, honey, and salt. Whisk together until blended. Taste, and add a little more honey if it's too tart. Remember - you can always add more honey to sweeten things up, but it's tough to take it away if you end up with too much sweetness in your dressing!

4. Lightly drizzle the dressing over the salad, toss it, and serve immediately.

- **Sheet Pan Baked Shrimp and Veggies**

Total Time: 25 min

Servings: 4-6

Ingredients

- 1 lb asparagus, tough parts removed, cut into 2-inch pieces
- 2 cups cherry tomatoes
- One red onion halved and thickly sliced
- 1 lb large shrimp, peeled and deveined
- Private Reserve Greek extra virgin olive oil
- ½ lemon, juice of
- Fresh chopped parsley for garnish

For the Sauce

- ⅓ cup Private Reserve Greek extra virgin olive oil
- ¼ cup white wine vinegar
- 1 tsp fresh grated ginger
- 1 tsp ground sumac
- 1 tsp ground cumin
- 1 tsp salt
- ½ tsp garlic powder

- ½ tsp ground black pepper

Description

1. Preheat your oven to 400 F. Pour all the sauce ingredients into a small bowl and stir with a wooden spoon.
2. Lay out the vegetables on the largest sheet pan you can find. On top of the veggies, pour about ¼ cup of the sauce and work to combine the sauce all together until all sides have been sufficiently sauced up. Spread out in a single layer, then bake in an oven for 10-12 minutes or until they're crisp but tender at the same time!
3. In a separate mixing bowl, add the cooked shrimp. Pour the remaining sauce on top and give it a good mix to ensure that each of the pieces of shrimp is evenly coated with the sauce.
4. Take vegetables out of the oven. Put half of the vegetables on one side of a pan, and put the shrimp on the other side. Leave enough space between the shrimp so that they don't touch. If crowded, they will not cook properly.
5. Put the pan back in the oven and bake for about 5 minutes until the shrimp is done. Be careful, not over-bake.
6. Once fully cooked, remove it from the oven. You can add a finishing touch of fresh lemon juice and chopped parsley leaves for additional flavor. Serve this with rice or your favorite side grain, and enjoy!

- **Roasted Cauliflower and Farro Salad with Feta and Avocado**

Prep Time: 15 minutes

Cook Time: 30 minutes

Servings: 4

Ingredients

- ⅓ cup pitted Kalamata olives, rinsed, half sliced into small rounds, and the rest halved lengthwise
- ¼ cup oil-packed sun-dried tomatoes, rinsed and roughly chopped
- ½ cup crumbled feta (about 2 ounces)
- One tablespoon lemon juice (about ½ lemon), plus more for serving
- Freshly ground black pepper, to taste
- One avocado, sliced into thin strips
- 4+ handfuls of leafy greens (spring greens, spinach, arugula, or baby kale are all excellent choices)

For the Roasted cauliflower

- One large head cauliflower (about 2 pounds), cut into bite-sized florets
- Two tablespoons extra-virgin olive oil
- ¼ teaspoon red pepper flakes (scale back or omit if sensitive to spice)
- ¼ teaspoon fine sea salt

For the Garlicky Farro

- 1 cup uncooked farro, rinsed
- Two teaspoons extra-virgin olive oil
- Two cloves garlic, pressed or minced
- ¼ teaspoon fine sea salt

Description

1. To roast the cauliflower florets, first preheat the oven to 425 F. Pour a generous amount of olive oil on top of the cauliflower florets and sprinkle them with red pepper flakes and a little bit of salt. Stir it around so that all sides are covered before putting it in an even layer in the pan. One can leave it for about 25 to 35 minutes until soft and golden in places on the edges.

2. Cooking the Farro: Rinse the pearled farro in a colander and drain it. Combine with three cups of water in a medium saucepan, and bring to a gentle boil. Then reduce the heat to a simmer and cook for 15 minutes, or until tender to the bite but still pleasantly chewy. Drain the excess water, add olive oil, garlic powder, salt & pepper; set aside.

3. Toss together your roasted cauliflower and cooked farro in a large serving bowl. Add the olives, sun-dried tomatoes, lemon juice, and feta cheese. Drizzle with sour cream and lemon juice. Season with salt and pepper if you desire.

4. Divide the avocados and greens between four large-sized plates. Top with a considerable amount of cauliflower and farro salad. Finish with an extra drizzle of olive oil or squeeze lemon juice, depending on your taste preference. Serve promptly!

- **Greek Chickpea Stew**

Prep Time: 10 Min

Prep Time: 2hrs

Servings: 2

Ingredients

- One cup dry chickpeas 9 oz or 250 gms soaked, rinsed, and peeled).
- One large onion diced
- One garlic clove cut in half
- One bay leaf
- ¼ cup olive oil
- salt/pepper
- lemon for serving
- optional: parsley or oregano for serving

Description

1. Place the chickpeas in a pot, cover them with water, and bring to a boil. Remove the chickpeas, rinse and place them again in a clean pot to ensure that they are safe from contaminating other foods once you're finished cleaning.
2. Chop the onion, garlic, and Bay leaves until fine. Add in ¼tsp salt and some Olive Oil to the chickpeas. Add your water until you can see three-quarters of an inch of water above the top of the beans.
3. Simmer for about two to three hours until it's soft and mushy.
4. Serve with a drizzle of extra-virgin olive oil and plenty of freshly ground black pepper.

- **Creamy Wild Rice Soup**

Ready in 1hr 15 min.

Ingredients

- 4 cups vegetable stock
- 1 (8-ounce) package button mushrooms, trimmed and quartered
- ¾ cup uncooked wild rice, rinsed and drained
- ½ cup thinly sliced leek (white part only)
- Four cloves garlic, minced
- 1 cup chopped red bell pepper
- ½ cup chopped carrot
- ¼ teaspoon sea salt
- ¼ cup almond flour
- ¼ cup chickpea flour
- One tablespoon snipped fresh thyme
- One tablespoon white wine vinegar

Description

1. Combine your ingredients (stock, garlic, wild rice, mushrooms, wild rice, and leek) in a soup pot.
2. Bring all the ingredients you've brought together to a boil. Then reduce the heat to medium-low and simmer until the rice is tender. That comes out to about 45-50 minutes or so as long as you have some water in your boiling pot.
3. Add in the bell peppers, carrot, and sprinkle of salt, then cover and simmer for about 8 minutes more, depending on what you prefer.
4. Mix the almond and chickpea flours; add in ¼ cup water. Stir until you create a paste-like texture or bubbly, about 1-2 minutes.
5. To reach your desired consistency, you can stir up to ½ cup more water. And! Stir in vinegar and thyme.

• Kimchi Brown Rice Bliss Bowls

Prep Time: 10 min

Cook Time: 30 min

Serves: 2-3

Ingredients

- 1 cup cooked brown rice
- Heaping ¼ cup kimchi
- 1 Persian cucumber, peeled into ribbons
- ½ cup thinly sliced red cabbage
- ½ avocado, sliced
- 8 ounces Marinated Tempeh, Baked or Grilled
- ½ recipe Peanut Sauce
- ½ teaspoon sesame seeds

- 2 Thai chiles, thinly sliced, optional
- Lime slices, for serving
- Microgreens, for garnish, optional

Description

1. Combine the bowls with cabbage, rice, avocado, kimchi, cucumber, and tempeh.
2. Drizzle generously with peanut sauce, sprinkle with sesame seeds, and top with cooling Thai chiles if desired. Serve with lime wedges on the side, along with the remaining peanut sauce. Garnish the dish with microgreens because your taste buds will be able to handle it.

CHAPTER NINE: HOW TO CONVINCE YOUR PARTNER TO START A PLANT-BASED LIFESTYLE

Certain lifestyle changes come naturally to us - like not engaging in violence or unplugging electronics to save energy - but other changes take some getting used to. One such change is going vegan; many people consider themselves "vegetarian" instead of fully committed vegans who eliminate all animal products from their diet.

No matter how compatible you think, the two of you may be, suggesting that your partner should consider going vegan can spark some intense reactions. Our partners can feel very strongly about what they put in their mouths, and we want to make sure they feel included when we decide to take a step towards being cruelty-free. Sometimes when a carnivore is faced with dining next to us without any flesh, they will often become somewhat defensive and dig their heels in claiming that animals eating meat are natural because they are on top of the food chain and not partly rationalizing it by pointing out that humans are technically omnivores too...Fear not! There are ways that one may persuade their significant other to adopt a compassionate lifestyle, simply by trying out various ideas and methods permissible within ethical and moral standards, of course. Moreover, here are some simple tips to get your partner on board the vegan lifestyle so both of you can successfully bring forth the desired outcome!

I.   Start by educating yourself and your partner on the benefits of a plant-based diet.

While your partner will most likely have a negative attitude towards the idea of going vegan, the benefits of the lifestyle are also very appealing. It's a great idea to show your partner how you're already healthy and how you're saving money on animal products. If your partner is already a meat-eater, it's important to show them that you're a vegan.

By presenting facts that prove that being vegan is healthy for the planet and the animals, your partner will be more likely to join you. Many resources are available online, and you can even find documentaries or books on the topic. Plant-based diets such as Veganism are rich in fruits, vegetables, whole grains, nuts, and seeds rich in antioxidants, phytonutrients, dietary fiber, healthy fats, which are helpful towards having a healthy heart, reduced risk of developing Type 2 diabetes, Cancer. Plant-based foods also help in losing weight, help in saving the environment, and rescuing animals from the cruelty of humankind.

II.   Make gradual changes to your diet instead of going cold turkey.

Truth be told, you can't turn someone into a vegan in one day! Make small gradual changes to your diet. This will make the transition easier for both of you and give your partner time to get used to the idea. You can start by incorporating more fruits and vegetables into your diet than processed foods. Then you can incorporate whole grains like oats, quinoa, brown rice instead of brown rice, or even drink water instead of soda. The point is to take baby steps towards adopting a Vegan diet because it will take time before your partner makes the switch to a Vegan lifestyle.

III.   Be open about your eating habits.

If you can talk openly with your partner, it will make them feel comfortable discussing their concerns or questions about the vegan diet. Dispel the common myths and misconceptions about the vegan diet, such as the myth that Vegans can't get enough proteins from plant-based foods.

Also, talk about the shortcomings of a Vegan diet and recommend supplementation for nutrients that you cannot get enough of when you're on a Vegan diet. Such nutrients include Vitamin B12, Calcium, Vitamin D, and so on.

IV.   Make sure that the new diet is sustainable for both of you.

The best diet is one that is sustainable and doesn't run you dry. Vegetarian or vegan diets are both sustainable when they come to the land required for food. If done right, a meatless diet won't suffer because then it will be considered virtuous in terms of its sustainability. But if you stay with the same meals all year, your plan on what kind of lifestyle you want to adopt might not go as smoothly as you think. To avoid eating the same meals year-round, develop a meal plan together and shop for groceries as a team instead of individually doing all the work on your own.

V.   Be positive about your new lifestyle!

When you present your partner with the idea that they should go vegan, first identify that you're there to help them because you love them and are concerned about their health. Ask what it is they're struggling with and seek a way to identify parallels between whatever they want eating animal products is not providing for and a switch in lifestyle.

This will encourage your partner to support you in the changes you're making for yourself and their future. You can share your plant-based recipes with your family as well. They might join your new lifestyle sooner than you think.

VI.   Be patient and open to suggestions from your partner.

Just because they aren't as enthusiastic about the new diet as you are doesn't mean that they don't support you! If they suggest something, contemplate it rather than dismiss their opinion outright. Your loved ones want to see you happy with whatever changes you make in your life, so try to work together as a team.

Now you can get inspired by celebrities too! Finding inspiration is not always easy, but for a lot of people, it helps to look at their role models and see how they do things. As the world has become more and more digitally connected, there are now more options than ever before. So if you're looking for celebrity quotes and inspiration, then read on.

Plant-based eating has been around since the beginning of time, and it's continuing to grow in popularity. Celebrities such as Beyonce, Ellie Goulding, Liam Hemsworth, and many more have embraced this way of life and are even spreading the word about its benefits.

When it comes to plant-based diets, there are different ways to go about it. You can either choose to be vegan or vegetarian. Vegan celebrities avoid all animal products, including dairy and eggs, while vegetarians still consume these items. Plant-based diets have been linked to reduced risk for chronic diseases such as cancer, heart disease, and diabetes. Plant-based diets offer better skin complexion, improved cardiovascular health, weight loss or maintenance, enhanced energy, and vitality. They are also great for the environment!

Celebrities That Eat a Plant-Based Diet and How They Do It

If you're looking for celebrity examples of a plant-based diet, there are many to choose from. Natalie Portman, the wife of environmentalist Bill Clinton, is a strong advocate for the diet. She loved McDonald's and ate it every day but has since stopped after learning about the benefits. Kirsten Bell is the popular vegan magazine Naked Food and recently went vegan with her husband, Dax Shepard.

Actor Maggie Q is a strong advocate for the plant-based diet, and she has been a vegetarian from birth. In the documentary "Eating You Alive" (released in 2016), she talks about the harmful effects of eating animal products and how to prevent chronic diseases through a plant-based diet. Joss Stone, who has embraced a plant-based diet since childhood, has said that she sang Amazing Grace to cows to feel more alive.

Emma Stone is an activist and a long-time vegetarian. In her late 20s, she was suffering from acne and had a lack of energy. A female stranger suggested she try adopting a vegan diet for better skin. After trying it, she became a vegan and kept her diet strictly plant-based. Other plant-based celebs include Pamela Anderson, Diane Keaton, Sarah Silverman, and Tobe Moquin. She has also been a strict vegetarian since she was 12 years old.

Woody Harrelson is another celebrity who tries to stay healthy and active. Despite being nearly 60 years old, she still looks young, despite her age. She has been Vegan for almost three years and has never eaten meat! She is a shining example of a healthy and active lifestyle! It is not just her body that inspires a generation to go vegan.

Some celebrities are vegan and vegetarian. Some are even vocal about social issues. For instance, Jared Leto is a vegan and a spokesperson for animal rights. The actress credits her plant-based diet and yoga for her youthful and lean body. He has also embraced a plant-based diet. She is one of the most prominent celebrities who follows a plant-based diet.

In addition to the food choices, celebrities who practice a plant-based diet have more energy and feel better overall. Rusty Rose has a plant-based diet and gives up coffee for the environment. Alicia Silverstone is a vegan, a vegetarian, and a devoted animal lover. And more celebrities make the plant-based diet a lifestyle.

Other famous people who practice a plant-based diet include Julia Roberts, Ruby Rose, and Lizzo. Unlike many other famous people, these celebrities have all decided to eat a plant-based diet to remain healthy. They do this not only for ethical reasons but also for practical reasons and to help the environment. While they are not strictly vegan, they are not opposed to it.

Several celebrities have become vegan in recent years. This is an excellent thing for the environment. Most vegan celebrities do their part to help the environment, and many use their platform to advocate for animal rights. Like Millie Bobby Brown, some famous people have been vegetarian for 15 years and have recently switched to a primarily raw vegan diet. While these celebs may be the most famous example of a plant-based diet, they have all been able to keep their youth and beauty for years.

The best thing about plant-based celebrities is that they provide an example for all of us. If more people in our society could adopt a plant-based diet, it would revolutionize our food industry and improve everyone's health in many ways. Ultimately, people like this should be the best role models in our society, and they are here to show that a plant-based diet is good for you and very enjoyable.

So, what do these celebrities eat daily? Here is a list of some common foods that they consume:

- Fruits and vegetables

- Whole grains

- Beans and legumes

- Nuts and seeds

- Plant-based protein powders

As you can see, plant-based diets are a great way to improve your overall health, and they also taste amazing! Celebrities such as Liam Hemsworth have been practicing this lifestyle for years now, along with Beyonce, who recently changed her diet. Plant-Based is the new black!

CHAPTER TEN: MISTAKES TO AVOID ON A PLANT-BASED LIFESTYLE TO MAKE SURE YOU'RE SUCCESSFUL

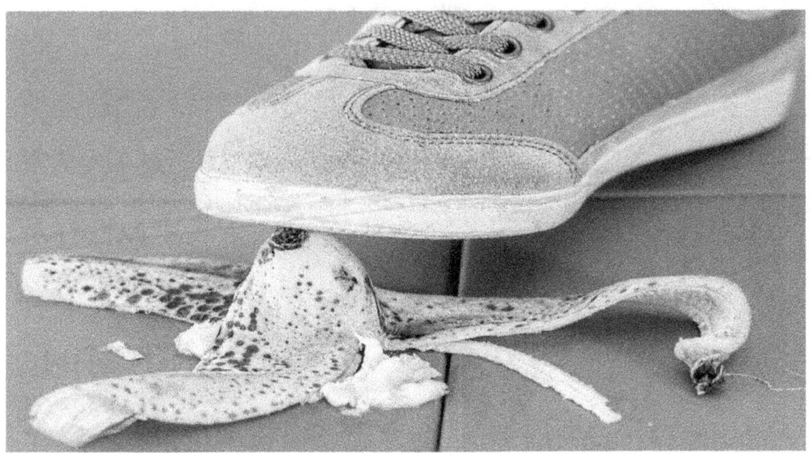

Have you decided to transition to a plant-based diet but don't know where to start? Or perhaps, you've started the diet but quickly fell off track?

While it is essential to focus on whole foods sources, plant-based diets can sometimes be challenging to follow. While packaged foods make meal preparation easier and provide quick and convenient meals, a plant-based diet advocate should avoid relying too heavily on such foods. For example, although processed meat and snacks are easy to grab, many are high in fat and contain potentially harmful ingredients.

Changing your diet to a plant-based diet can be difficult, but it is also possible to reap the benefits. A plant-based diet is low in calories and is incredibly easy to incorporate into your daily routine. As long as you follow the food list that is available to you and follow the nutritional guidelines, you'll be on your way to a healthier lifestyle in no time. Let's look at some common ways people have faltered or have been unsuccessful in this lifestyle.

1. **Relying on a plant-based diet without eating a balanced diet.**

While it may sound like a healthy diet, it's important to remember that a plant-based diet should be a lifestyle change, not a dietary restriction. Using a balance of proteins, carbohydrates, and fats can help you avoid the health risks that are associated with not consuming a balanced diet. Get all your plant-based proteins right, get the right sources of carbohydrates, consume the healthy fats, drink water, eat plenty of fruits and vegetables to get the recommended daily amount of vitamins and minerals.

2. **Skipping breakfast to lose weight faster.**

Breakfast is the most important meal of the day. Some people skip breakfast to lose weight faster. But this will leave your body deficient of the nutrients you need to perform the activities of the day. The plant-based diet is supposed to be easy to transition to, but changing habits is always a challenge. The plant-based diet can help you lose weight without skipping meals because they're less in calories, they're rich in fiber which makes you feel full quicker and for longer. If you are a beginner, it is good to be patient and not rush into it, weight loss takes time. When starting a plant-based diet, you may experience initial hunger, irritability, and fatigue, but eventually, you will feel better. The first few weeks after switching to a plant-based diet will take a few weeks or even months to kick-start the process.

3. **Poor knowledge.**

It's a common misconception to believe that a plant-based diet is easy to follow. However, the fact is that it is not easy. For example, a plant-based diet requires you to adjust to a new way of eating and learn new ways of preparing it.

As a plant-based diet, you shouldn't have trouble incorporating meat and processed food into your diet. While you won't be missing out on meat, a plant-based diet should not cause you to crave meat or processed foods. While it is easy to switch to a plant-based diet, you should be patient. During this time, you may feel irritable and tired. Nevertheless, most people will feel much better once they ditch processed foods.

While the concept of a plant-based diet sounds straightforward, the reality is that there are many things you need to know to succeed.

Drinking at least 64 ounces of water a day is essential, but don't forget to avoid the temptation to consume meat if you want to make the transition successfully. A plant-based diet does not exclude meat, but it reduces your intake.

4. Poor Food Preparation

When it comes to eating your plant-based diet, you must pay special attention to how the foods are prepared. The most effective way to preserve these nutrients is to steam them for at least 5 minutes. Keep in mind that a plant-based diet is an excellent choice for your health. It is a good choice for those who wish to feel better and enjoy more energy and vitality.

You should also avoid cooking too oily foods such as fatty foods and fried foods, and foods low in fiber. Foods that are too oily can be high in unhealthy fats. Foods high in fiber are essential for your health and your body's well-being. A vegan diet should only contain the foods you like and are not too expensive.

5. Not getting enough protein.

There are many reasons for starting a plant-based lifestyle. For some, the main reason is for health reasons. Others are looking to improve their body, mind, and soul. And others still have an emotional attachment to the animals they've come to love. Getting enough protein is just as important as getting enough calories. Most experts agree that protein is one of the primary components of a healthy body. Eating too little protein will result in muscle loss and slower weight loss.

Moreover, it is crucial for overall health to get adequate protein intake. Eating too much protein can lead to kidney problems, heartburn, and constipation. Eating the right amount of protein will ensure that you stay satisfied, have fewer cravings, and feel as full during a meal.

A great way to get enough protein on a plant-based diet is to focus on:

- **Legumes**

Many legumes are packed with protein, such as lentils, beans, peas, edamame/soybeans (and products made from soy: tofu, tempeh, etc.), and peanuts. These delicious and nutritious foods are packed with protein, making them an important part of any plant-based diet.

- **Whole grains**

 Kamut, Teff, Wheat, Quinoa, Rice, Wild Rice, Millet, Oats, and Buckwheat have you covered!

- **Nuts and Seeds**

A nutritious and protein-packed snack option, nuts and seeds like almonds, cashews, and walnuts are a great way to fuel your body. Hazelnuts, pecans, hemp seeds, pumpkin seeds, sunflower seeds, flax seeds, sesame seeds, and chia seeds are also great protein sources.

- **Fruits and Vegetables**

Corn, broccoli, asparagus, brussels sprouts, and artichokes are some examples of vegetables and fruits that contain higher protein levels than other plant-based foods.

6. Not getting enough magnesium.

About 90 percent of the world's magnesium comes from plants. Other nutrients, such as iron and zinc, also come from plants. The best sources of magnesium include dark green leafy vegetables, nuts, and whole grains. Although you can get most of your magnesium from plant-based foods, vegan people need to take more. Studies show that the average diet is about 10 percent magnesium deficient. Therefore, if you're a vegan, you can add extra magnesium to your diet.

7. Not getting enough B vitamins.

Vegetarians should also consider the possibility of deficiency of B vitamins.

- **Vitamin B1**

The nutrient vitamin B1 is responsible for turning food into energy, and it's found in plant-based foods such as whole-grain cereals, yeast, beans, nuts, and meat can provide vitamin B1 for those not on a strict vegan diet. A lack of B1 can lead to the debilitating disease beriberi, impacting the heart, digestive, and nervous systems.

Did you know that the recommended daily intake of vitamin B1 is different for men and women? For women over 18, the recommended intake is 1.1-1.4 mg, while for men aged 14 and older, the recommended intake is 1.2 mg.

- **Vitamin B2 (Riboflavin)**

Riboflavin is a water-soluble vitamin that is essential in the human diet. It helps the body metabolize food into energy and also helps keep the skin, gut, and blood cells healthy. Getting enough riboflavin may help prevent migraine headaches cataracts and boost the immune system. It can also treat acne, muscle cramps, and energy levels.

You can get your daily dose of Vitamin B2 from various natural sources, such as nuts, green vegetables, meat, and dairy products. Did you know that you need only 1.3 mg of vitamin B2 each day if you're a man and 1.1 mg if you're a woman? Pregnant women need 1.4 mg, and breastfeeding mothers should have 1.6 mg.

- **Vitamin B3 (Niacin)**

Niacin is essential for energy production in the body. It helps convert food components into usable energy. Good sources of niacin include legumes, nuts, enriched bread, dairy, fish, and lean meats.

You need at least 14 mg of Vitamin B3 each day if you're a girl aged 14 or older; boys in this age group need 16 mg.

- **Vitamin B5 (Pantothenic acid)**

Pantothenic acid is essential for energy production and hormone synthesis in the body. It also helps drive many biochemical reactions in the cells, including the breakdown of carbohydrates and lipids.

You can find vitamin B5 in various foods, including broccoli, kale, avocado, whole-grain cereals, potatoes, dairy, and organ meats. Getting 5 mg of vitamin B5 each day is recommended for all people age 14 and older.

- **Vitamin B6 (Pyridoxine)**

The health benefits of vitamin B6 are vast; it helps keep the immune system functioning properly, aids in normal brain development, and even helps keep our nervous system healthy and in check. This important vitamin is found in many common foods, such as poultry, fish, potatoes, chickpeas, and bananas.

You should aim to consume 1.3 mg of vitamin B6 per day if you are an adult aged 50 or below. However, pregnant or breastfeeding teens and women need up to 2 mg per day to meet their nutritional needs.

- **Vitamin B12**

This is a water-soluble vitamin that isn't found in many plant foods. Vitamin B12 is required for healthy nervous system function, proper energy levels, red blood cell formation, and more. An adequate intake of B12 is important for the optimal functioning of the central nervous system and the immune system. The body also requires Vitamin B12 for red blood cell formation and proper DNA synthesis. You can get your daily dose of vitamin B12 from many vegan-friendly foods fortified with nutrients, such as plant milk, soy products, and breakfast cereals. Additionally, Vitamin B12 supplements are a great way to ensure you're getting enough of the nutrient. Those who don't follow strict plant-based eating like the vegan diet, fish, dairy products, eggs, meat, and poultry are excellent animal sources of vitamin B12.

You only need 2.4 micrograms of vitamin B12 each day, but pregnant or breastfeeding teens and women need more - 2.6 to 2.8 mcg daily. If you are not sure if you are Vitamin B12 deficient, ask your doctor to test your blood.

8. Not getting enough calcium.

If you are vegan, chances are you're low in calcium. Calcium is important for proper energy production, muscle contraction, blood clotting, and neurotransmitter and hormone production. It is found in fortified foods such as tofu, kale, broccoli, collard greens, legumes, seeds, and grains. Some supplements may contain calcium as well. Canned sardines and salmon with bones are some animal sources of calcium.

According to WHO, 500 to 700 mg of calcium per day is recommended.

Many studies have shown that not getting enough calcium can lead to many health problems. According to the Linus Pauling Institute, it's estimated that 35 percent of Americans aren't getting enough calcium. To prevent bone fractures, you can also take a calcium supplement.

9. Not getting enough zinc.

Zinc is essential for proper immune system function, brain and nervous system development, wound healing, growth and development of teeth and bones, reproduction, and more. This mineral is found in fortified foods, whole grains, beans, nuts, and legumes. Oysters, red meat, and poultry are some animal sources of zinc. Zinc is a mineral that is essential in small amounts but can have adverse effects when taken in high doses for long periods. These can include suppressed immunity, decreased HDL levels, anemia, and copper deficiency.

You should aim to consume 8 milligrams of zinc per day if you're a woman and 11 milligrams if you're a man.

10. Not getting enough iron.

Iron is essential for proper energy production, oxygen transportation, and red blood cell formation, among other things. It is best obtained through plant-based foods or supplements.

Good sources of iron include beans, lentils, mushrooms, fortified milk, tofu, and dark green leafy vegetables. Red meats, poultry, offal, fish, eggs are some animal sources of iron.

Too little iron can leave you exhausted and decrease your immune function due to anemia.

Adult men and post-menopausal women need only 8 mg of iron per day. 18 mg is the recommended dose for adult women, and pregnant women should shoot for 27 mg per day.

There are two types of iron: heme and non-heme. Heme iron is only found in animal products, while non-heme iron is found in plants. Your body more easily absorbs heme iron than non-heme iron. Some people recommend that vegans aim for 1.8 times the normal RDA, but more studies are needed to establish whether high intakes are necessary.

11. Not consuming the good fats needed for an active and healthy life.

Good fats are important for keeping your organs functioning properly, having healthy skin and hair, and helping your body absorb important vitamins. The three main types of dietary fats include; unsaturated, saturated, and trans fats. Saturated fats are typically solid at room temperature, and most nutrition experts recommend limiting saturated fat intake to prevent an imbalance that can lead to harmful LDL cholesterol and blockages in arteries. Sources of saturated fat include red meat, whole milk, cheese, coconut oil, and many commercially prepared baked goods. Trans fats are a type of unhealthy fat found in dairy products and meats. However, they are also often found in hydrogenated vegetable oils and processed foods. Trans fats raise LDL (bad cholesterol) levels while lowering HDL (good cholesterol). Additionally, trans fats are associated with a higher risk of heart disease, obesity, and type 2 diabetes. Unsaturated fats, on the other hand, can have beneficial effects on your body by decreasing LDL ("bad") cholesterol and increasing HDL ("good") cholesterol levels.

There are many different types of omega-3 fatty acids, but alpha-linolenic acid (ALA) is the only one that is essential- you can only get it from your diet. The long-chain omega-3 fatty acids, EPA and DHA, are not essential, but they do have many health benefits, so it's a good idea to include them in your diet whenever possible.The American Heart Association recommends limiting your daily fat intake to 25-35% of total calories and saturated fat to less than 7% of total calories for heart health. Aim for the following foods for your protein:

- **Nuts**

Adding nuts to your diet is a great way to get healthy fats and minerals into your body. Walnuts, almonds, pistachios, and pecans are great sources of unsaturated fats, omega-3 and omega-6 fatty acids, and other minerals. Brazil nuts and cashews are also great sources of fat, but they have a higher concentration of saturated fats.

- **Avocados**

Avocados are a nutritional powerhouse, providing a creamy, delicious way to add healthy fats to your diet. With 77% fat, most of it is monounsaturated; they're a great way to boost your nutrient intake. One medium avocado provides 21 grams of fat and vitamins, minerals, and antioxidants.

- **Coconut**

Coconut and coconut oil are a source of medium-chain triglycerides (MCTs). MCTs are a type of saturated fat that is easier for the liver to break down and convert into energy or ketones. MCTs help curb hunger, keep you satiated for longer, and reduce calorie consumption.

- **Flaxseeds**

Flaxseeds are a great source of plant-based omega3 fatty acids. In just one tablespoon, you can get up to 1.8 grams of omega 3s. Add them to your favorite smoothie, granola bars, or morning oats for a healthy and delicious crunch.

- **Extra Virgin Olive Oil**

Extra-virgin olive oil is a nutritional powerhouse, providing a rich source of polyunsaturated fatty acids, including omega-6 and omega-3 fatty acids. A single tablespoon of this healthful oil packs in 14 grams of fat, making it a valuable addition to any diet.

12. Not getting enough Vitamin D.

This is a fat-soluble vitamin that is important for optimal health, including promoting healthy bones and teeth and the proper function of the immune system.

You can get Vitamin D from the sun, but it's also found in foods. This vitamin is found in some plant-based foods like mushrooms, fortified foods, and fortified milk. But be careful with your intake of vitamin D supplements since this can cause a condition called hypervitaminosis D. Fish, offal, egg, dairy products, and meat are some animal sources of vitamin D.

The best way to get your daily dose of vitamin D is by taking 400 international units (IU) if you are 12 months or younger, 600 IU if you are between the ages of 1 and 70, and 800 IU if you are over 70.

13. Not getting enough Potassium.

Potassium is important for proper bodily functions and muscle contraction. It is found in fruits and vegetables and some fortified foods like potato products. Fish, poultry, and meats can provide calcium too.

Despite the lack of an RDA for potassium, many organizations recommend consuming at least 3,500 mg per day through food.

14. Not getting enough Iodine.

Getting enough iodine is crucial for healthy thyroid function, which controls your metabolism. Without enough iodine, you may develop hypothyroidism (low thyroid function). Symptoms of hypothyroidism include fatigue, brain fog, weight gain, and hair loss.

Foods with high iodine levels include iodized salt, seafood, seaweed, and dairy products. Vegans not getting enough iodine from seaweed or iodized salt should consider taking an iodine supplement. The RDA for iodine is 150 mcg per day for adults. If you're pregnant, you should aim for 220 mcg per day.

Those breastfeeding are recommended further to increase their daily intake to 290 mcg per day. Children aged 1 to 3 years old should have 90 mcg of iodine per day, while those aged 4 to 8 should have 130 mcg.

15. Not getting enough Vitamin C (Ascorbic acid)

The nutrient you need for strong bones and healthy muscles is Vitamin C. This vitamin is essential for healing wounds and forming new tissue. Many plant-based foods are good sources of vitamin C, including lemons, grapefruits, cantaloupe, spinach, red peppers, broccoli, tomatoes, kiwi, blackberries, and strawberries. Vitamin C is also found in fortified foods such as orange juice and fruits. Though vitamin C is not found in high quantities in cooked animal foods, it can still be acquired through other means. Raw liver, fish roe, and eggs are all great sources of nutrients and raw meat and fish.

Adult Recommended Daily Amount of Vitamin C is 65-90 milligrams.

CHAPTER ELEVEN: PLANT-BASED DIET FOR ATHLETES

Find Out How a Plant-Based Diet Can Fuel Your Body To Improve Your Athletic Performance, Make You Feel Energized, Build Your Muscles, Make You Lose Weight And Boost Your Confidence.

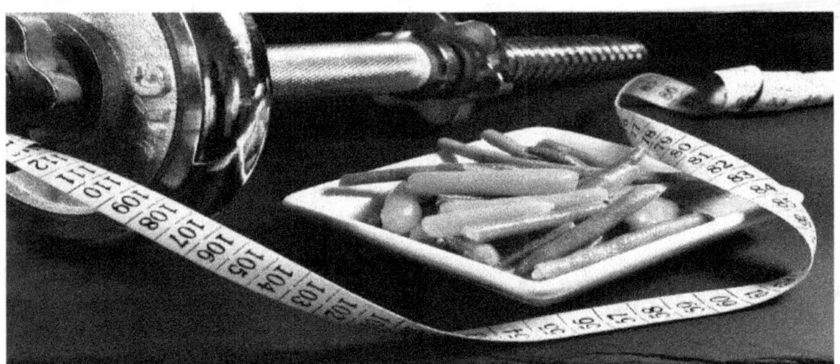

Whether it was because of my love for animals, my desire to protect the environment, or my health, I have been thinking about becoming a vegetarian for years. In 2011, I decided to try it out. I had my hesitations and worries, which were directed at myself. I questioned, "If I stop eating meat and eggs, how would I get enough protein?" "Would I have enough energy to compete and maintain my lifestyle?"

Running is my favorite recreational activity; however, I always found it hard to hit my stride over the years. Since switching diets, I've seen a tremendous improvement in my athletic performance. Nowadays, thanks to an improved diet and workout routine, I rarely get injured, and training has become so much easier.

A plant-based diet is not unlike a healthy one, so there isn't much you've got to do besides cut out the meat and animal products that people on a 'plant-based' diet aim to limit. Sure, we realize how hard it can be to let go of your daily dose of bacon and sausage, but if you eat more whole foods in the first place, then making small changes like doing so should feel natural.

Are you an athlete looking for a way to power up your performance? A plant-based diet could be the answer! A growing number of professional athletes have turned to a whole-foods, plant-based diet to reach optimal performance. Colin Kaepernick, Venus Williams, United States soccer star Alex Morgan, professional surfer Tia Blanco, WNBA player and four-time Olympic gold medalist Diana Taurasi, and dozens more pros are all vegan.

Athletes train more rigorously than the average person and regularly push their bodies to their limits, especially if they are involved in physically demanding sports. As such, they must fuel their bodies with nourishing food. A Plant-Based Diet is a great choice for athletes because it boosts energy and improves athletic performance. In addition, a plant-based diet can help you recover from an intense workout faster and minimize sickness. If you want to learn more about the benefits of eating a plant-based diet to an athlete, read on!

A plant-based diet is perfect for athletes and others who want to get in shape. It's important to note that it is not a short-term goal. This diet is a lifestyle change for those who want to get fit and lose weight. It is important to find a diet that works for you and is compatible with your goals. A plant-based diet is the best option for athletes looking to achieve their fitness goals.

Recent research has shown that athletes who switch to a plant-based diet can see decreases in weight, create leaner bodies, and improve stamina. A plant-based diet is not the only way to achieve better performance, but it may be the best answer! Switching to a plant-based diet can not only help you lose weight and have a healthier BMI, but it can also make you leaner overall, as measured by your body's adiposity.

For example, the following athletes:

Cyclists. Cyclists who want to reduce weight can benefit from plant-based diets high in fiber and vitamins. Increasing fiber intake decreases blood sugar levels brings satiety, making it easier for cyclists to manage their health, weight, and energy throughout the race.

Climbers. Climbers must maintain the right body weight to climb at a high altitude and not be weighed down by additional body fat.

As an athlete, you need to balance the nutrients that you consume with the nutrients that your body needs. A plant-based diet can help you lose body fat, improve performance, and reduce recovery time. The diet also includes plenty of fresh fruits and vegetables. The benefits of a plant-based d t are endless. These foods are full of fiber antioxidants and can be found in any grocery store.

While some athletes aim to decrease body fat percentage, athletes need to get enough calories to optimize their athletic performance. Since athletes are doing more physical activity each day than the average person, they also need to consume more calories to match their energy expenditure. Body fat percentage is best measured using the skinfold method. This technique uses a pair of calipers to measure the subcutaneous fat thickness just below the skin. Combining two or more of these measurements (triceps, biceps, subscapular, abdominal) allows the calculation of body fat percentage with reasonable accuracy. Measurements should be taken on the same part of the body each time to compare data over time.

Here Are Some Tips for Athletes Starting a Plant-Based Diet.

1. Starting a Plant-Based Diet is not an All-Or-Nothing affair.

It can be easy to get confused about the term "plant-based diet." Many people automatically assume that they have to avoid meat, poultry, fish, eggs, and dairy altogether to go plant-based. While I strongly recommend you eliminate all animal products from your diet because they are no good for you (no matter the amounts), the trend is not necessarily about eliminating these foods entirely but rather incorporating them less frequently. For example, an athlete who follows a healthy diet may consume fish or eggs only once or twice a week at most, depending on how serious their training regime is. Athletes who opt for a plant-based diet may feel they have to avoid animal products 100% and often feel overwhelmed by the idea.

2. Make Small and Realistic Changes

When you transition to a plant-based diet as an athlete, it can feel like you are on a completely different planet! All the information can be overwhelming, but there are great resources that you can use to make the transition smooth.

The best way to eat a plant-based diet for athletes is by making small changes to the meals you already like! You don't want to make it too complicated because there are many tasty alternatives to the meats and animal products you've been using.

For example

You can start by adding avocado to your sandwiches in place of cheese. Avocado is a healthy fat, which will help you gain muscle, and it tastes amazing on a sandwich.

I'm a big fan of plant-based diets! A plant-based diet is something that many professional athletes are starting to use more often now as they realize they can still get all the protein they need and more by eating only plants! By taking snacks like cheese crackers and potato chips and replacing them with something like fresh fruit and nuts, you can keep snacking on things you already enjoy while making it a little healthier!

Replace your fries with salad once in a while, and instead of eating an extra piece of chicken for dinner, try ordering extra veggies! Tally how many servings you eat per day and add an extra 1 or 2 servings onto that number.

If you lag on various plant dishes, try one new dish that fits your taste buds and culinary preferences, such as lentils, almonds, tofu, each week, and learn what cooking tools, spices, or other ingredients you need will need to prepare them.

3. Dietary Balance

When it comes to bodyweight maintenance, energy in must equal energy out. Translation: If you're trying to stay fit, then you need to burn fuel as a means of performing. So for athletes (who burn fuel as a means of performing) to maintain or gain muscle mass, eat adequate amounts of calories. On the other hand, a low-energy (calorie) intake for high-intensity exercise can result in loss of muscle mass, menstrual dysfunction, and loss of bone density. If you don't consume enough calories, your body will break down muscle tissue for fuel. Sounds good, though! Right? Wrong! Because your muscles are the basis of your physical fitness, which is why eating plenty of healthy foods like carbohydrates and proteins is key!

4. Carbohydrates For Your Energy Needs

There's a time and place to work out, but there's also a time and place not to work out. Hey, we're all busy! But it's important to remember that exercise plays an enormous role in keeping our bodies healthy, functioning properly, and combatting common ailments like high blood pressure, anxiety or migraines, or even breathing problems. Just make sure that you give your body enough rest to avoid 'over-training' yourself, which happens to athletes who train too much. Try reducing the training one day a week before it becomes a habit if this applies to you. Do yourself a favor, and don't burn out!

What if I told you that your hard-earned muscles could pack up and leave if you're not careful? Well, it's true. When there's a lag between the number of calories you consume and those you burn, there will be a negative gap in the energy balance - aka an energy deficit. This may lead to your muscles shrinking over time - no matter how long or tough your workouts are. So yes, your diet should count as well!

On average, people need 1,800 to 2,000 calories per day. However, competitive rowers or runners may need 2-3 times this amount of calories per day to fuel their workouts. The recommended caloric intake will be much higher in athletes than in normal-weight adults with such a high energy requirement.

A plant-based diet is key to maintaining energy and stamina throughout the day. By incorporating complex carbohydrates into your diet, you can ensure that you have the sustained energy you need to perform at your best. Carbs should be your main energy source, so always focus on eating complex carbs rather than simple carbs.

Complex carbohydrates are essential for enhancing athletic performance. These carbohydrates are the building blocks of glycogen and are important for endurance training. The body requires more complex carbohydrate fuel than simple carbohydrates. Therefore, a plant-based diet provides a steady source of energy. The plant-based diet is high in carbohydrates, low in fat, and rich in vitamins and minerals.

Complex carbs (such as whole grains, vegetables, and legumes) are slowly digested by the body and provide sustained energy throughout the day. Simple carbs (like white bread, sweets, and processed foods) digest quickly and often result in a blood sugar spike that leads to fatigue and energy crashes.

Many athletes find that high-fat, low-carb diets are detrimental to their training, as they impair normal energy pathways and limit energy production. However, by ensuring they have enough glucose and glycogen stores and following a plant-based diet, they can overcome these limitations. Athletes should eat at least 80% of their calories from plant-based sources.

5. Protein

Protein, which is made of strings of amino acids, plays an important role in building and maintaining the body. Your body cannot create tissues such as muscle without protein. For your body to build a variety of tissues, our body needs 20 different amino acids to repair and recover them at a rapid rate during physical exercise. Even though we can make 11 of these on our own, we still need them in our diet because mammals cannot produce nine essential amino acids on their own. These nine thus have to come from our diet. Many people think that only meat offers the necessary protein for an active lifestyle and good health overall. But that wasn't the case when our ancestors relied on animal sources only! A plant-based diet based on grains, legumes, and vegetables provides us with those particular amino acids flawlessly!

The average person has different protein requirements than athletes. This is because the recommended dietary allowance (RDA) for the average sedentary or lightly active adult is 0.8 grams per kilogram of body weight per day, which is enough to meet their needs! Some authorities believe that this might be insufficient for highly active adult athletes. Athletes need more protein than the average person to perform at their best. The recommended range is 1.4-2.0 grams per kilogram per day. Animal proteins are a great source of essential amino acids, but when you eat a variety of plant-based proteins throughout the day, you'll get all the essential amino acids you need, so don't worry.

Are you looking to increase your protein intake? Add some delicious soy products (tempeh, tofu, edamame), beans, lentils, nuts, seeds, and quinoa to your diet for an extra boost!

Adding protein powder made from peas and rice may be an efficient way to consume more protein after a workout. Protein supplements that feature sourced ingredients naturally are suitable for vegan athletes.

More Extra Protein For Athletes

Beans are a great source of protein for athletes who are on the go and need something filling and nutritious. Top your salads with various beans, many of which can be purchased in a can or sold dried at the supermarkets right next to the pasta. Even if preparing legumes at home may take more time and effort with soaking and boiling, they're also much more budget-friendly when you do so. These legumes have 7-10 grams per serving, and some even come flavored as well if you're looking for that extra kick without the added preservatives or fat!

If you're an athlete on the lookout for a post-workout snack with solid protein content, blend soft tofu or non-dairy milk with your favorite fruit. This will give you not only a quick meal but make sure you don't miss out on vital nutrients when trying to recover pre or post-workout.

If you're an athlete in need of more protein and caloric intake, tempeh is a great food to meet those needs. Marinated tempeh, grilled on a bun or added to pasta sauce, is the perfect food for any athlete looking to consume more protein with less fat.

If you need protein on the go, try convenient and straightforward supplements like nutrition bars and soy powder shakes which are quick and easy to take.

6. Fat

Healthy diets are recommended for athletes as they provide the energy and nutrients needed to perform at their best. Animal products are high in saturated fat, leading to heart disease, diabetes, weight gain, and other chronic conditions. Instead, focus on eating a balanced diet with plenty of fiber, vegetables, and healthy fats from nuts, seeds, and avocados.

Omega 3 Fatty Acids For Plant-Based Athletes

One of the most significant barriers to adopting a plant-based diet is a lack of information. However, this is changing, and there are some great benefits to a plant-based diet for athletes. The most crucial factor is consuming the right amount of omega-3 fatty acids. There are three essential fatty acids (EFAs) that your body cannot produce: linoleic acid, linolenic acid, and alpha-linolenic acid. To obtain these vital EFAs, you need to eat dietary fat. A plant-based diet is low in omega-3 fatty acids. This is the primary reason why many athletes lack essential nutrients. The dietary sources of omega-3 fatty acids for plant-based athletes are often inadequate. The best source of omega-3 fatty acids is fish. In general, fish is the best source of these nutrients. It also contains DHA and EPA. But it's essential to get enough protein. You should aim for at least 10 grams of EPA and 5 grams of DHA per day. Microalgae supplements are a good option if you're looking to maximize your performance.

A plant-based athlete needs to eat various foods rich in omega-3 fatty acids, including flax and hemp seeds. These fats are essential for athletes, as vegans are low in these essential fatty acids. They are also vital for healthy brain function and endurance. Thankfully, there are plenty of plant-based sources of these fatty acids, such as walnuts and hemp oil. Some nuts and seeds, like macadamia nuts, cashews, pistachios, almonds, walnuts, and sesame seeds, are naturally very high in the polyunsaturated omega-3 ALA.

There are a few things vegetarians can do to improve their omega-3 levels. Most importantly, eating foods rich in omega-3 fatty acids is a great way to improve your athletic performance and health. If you are vegan or vegetarian, consider incorporating seaweed and algae into your diet. These foods are highly nutritious, and they may also be helpful for your diet. Additionally, O3FA supplements for plant-based athletes will provide your body with the nutrients it needs.

7. Vitamins and Minerals You Need to Stay Healthy as a Plant-Based Athlete.

Eating a healthy plant-based diet is a great way to stay fit, but it's essential to keep your essential vitamins and minerals as well. Plants are naturally filled with many of these nutritional components, but you need to be aware of what is lacking in vegan products to maintain health at the gym.

- **Vitamin B12**

This is a water-soluble vitamin that isn't found in many plant foods. Vitamin B12 is required for healthy nervous system function, proper energy levels, red blood cell formation, and more. An adequate intake of B12 is vital for the optimal functioning of the central nervous system and the immune system. The body also requires Vitamin B12 for red blood cell formation and proper DNA synthesis. You can get your daily dose of vitamin B12 from many vegan-friendly foods fortified with nutrients, such as plant milk, soy products, and breakfast cereals. Additionally, B12 supplements are a great way to ensure you're getting enough of the nutrient. Those who don't follow strict plant-based eating like the vegan diet, fish, dairy products, eggs, meat, and poultry are excellent animal sources of vitamin B12.

- **Vitamin D**

This is a fat-soluble vitamin that is important for optimal health, including promoting healthy bones and teeth and the proper function of the immune system. You can get Vitamin D from the sun, but it's also found in foods. This vitamin is found in some plant-based foods like mushrooms, fortified foods, and fortified milk. But be careful with your intake of vitamin D supplements which can cause a condition called hypervitaminosis D. Fish, offal, egg, dairy products, and meat are some animal sources of vitamin D.

- **Iron**

Iron is essential for proper energy production, oxygen transportation, and red blood cell formation, among other things. It is best obtained through plant-based foods or supplements. Good sources of iron include beans, lentils, mushrooms, fortified milk, tofu, and dark green leafy vegetables. Red meats, poultry, offal, fish, eggs are some animal sources of Iron.

- **Zinc**

Zinc is essential for proper immune system function, brain and nervous system development, wound healing, growth and development of teeth and bones, reproduction, and more. This mineral is found in fortified foods, whole grains, beans, nuts, and legumes. Oysters, red meat, and poultry are some animal sources of zinc. Zinc is a mineral that is essential in small amounts but can have adverse effects when taken in high doses for long periods. These can include suppressed immunity, decreased HDL levels, anemia, and copper deficiency.

- **Calcium**

Calcium is essential for proper energy production, muscle contraction, blood clotting, and neurotransmitter and hormone production. It is found in fortified foods such as tofu, kale, broccoli, collard greens, legumes, seeds, and grains. Some supplements may contain calcium as well. Canned sardines and salmon with bones are some animal sources of calcium.

- **Potassium**

Potassium is vital for proper bodily functions and muscle contraction. It is found in fruits and vegetables and some fortified foods like potato products. Fish, poultry, and meats can provide calcium too.

- **Vitamin C (Ascorbic acid)**

The nutrient you need for strong bones and healthy muscles is Vitamin C. This vitamin is essential for healing wounds and forming new tissue. Many plant-based foods are good sources of vitamin C, including lemons, grapefruits, cantaloupe, spinach, red peppers, broccoli, tomatoes, kiwi, blackberries, and strawberries. Vitamin C is also found in fortified foods such as orange juice and fruits. Though vitamin C is not found in high quantities in cooked animal foods, it can still be acquired through other means. Raw liver, fish roe, and eggs are all great sources of nutrients and raw meat and fish.

- **Water**

Dehydration is not something you want to keep putting off or classifying as another thing you'll "deal with after that huge meeting" is over. Make sure you keep hydrated during the day and be sure to drink at least eight glasses of water daily so you can ward off headaches, fatigue, and heat intolerance. Dehydration causes cramps and exhaustion. And even death. So be sure you're staying hydrated adequately at every turn for peak performance!

Water is the best way to stay properly hydrated—especially if you're doing something physical like exercising. When you're working out, a lot of fluid gets depleted from your system. You'll be able to tell when you get thirsty in the middle of what you're doing because you'll feel that uncomfortable dry throat and tongue on your body. And those are just some of the many signs! If this happens, go ahead and drink up right away! Just make sure that you're drinking enough before too long. You can use the following guidelines for better hydration.

Exercise is crucial for all of us. Drinking water can be essential for those who don't find it easy to drink a lot at one go. 2 Hours before exercise, drink at least 14-20 ounces of fluid (preferably water). (1.75-2.5 cups)

While exercising, drink 5 to 12 ounces (1 to 1 1/2 cups) of fluid (preferably water) every 15 to 20 minutes.

After exercising, it's essential to drink plenty of water, especially if you lose weight in the process. If you have lost a considerable amount of weight, you will need 16-24 ounces for every pound lost during your exercise. Weigh yourself both before and after exercise so that you can be sure how much fluid would be appropriate to replace what was lost.

To sum up the athletic performance, remember that it's essential for athletes to eat healthy, nutritious foods that will help them perform at their best. Here are some quick tips on how to start eating healthier:

- **Fruits**

As an athlete, your body burns a lot of calories. The best way to ensure your body stays running at full capacity is essential to eat healthily. There are many vitamins and minerals that you need to ensure your body has enough of them to work at its best. If you were about to run a race, what would you choose? A bowl of ice cream or apples and carrots? Go for the options with more vitamins! You'll feel better during the race and less like crashing midway through! Fruit is especially rich in vitamins and minerals required for a healthy lifestyle.

- **Whole grains**

As an athlete, you should make sure that you have whole-grain bread, wholewheat rice and pasta, and granolas in your diet because they are rich in complex carbohydrates, fiber, zinc, and B vitamins. A single serving of each of these also provides about 2 to 3 grams of protein essential for energy recovery and cell growth.

- **Legumes**

As an athlete, it is strongly recommended that you choose a variety of legumes such as beans like chickpeas, black beans, kidney beans, soy milk, tofu, soybean curd, and textured vegetable protein.

- **Vegetables**

As an athlete, you'll need to choose colorful vegetables like bell peppers and carrots and leafy greens such as spinach and kale. These foods provide a variety of nutrients, including vitamin C and beta-carotene, which are vital for protecting the body against stress caused by intense exercise. Iron, calcium, fiber, and protein are also necessary for your diet to ensure that you're getting all the necessary nutrients!

- **Vitamin B12 Supplementation**

Athletes are encouraged not to forget the importance of vitamin B12 in their diets. Athletes at all levels should be training as hard as they possibly can. This makes it essential for athletes to ensure that they have all their basic nutritional requirements met before, during, and after their athletic performances. You will find that 2 - 3 times a week, some athletes would go to the extreme of taking a multivitamin supplement or even vitamin B12 to provide additional nourishment to their system. As an athlete, you can consider that fortified foods such as fortified cereal and soy or rice milk with cyanocobalamin (the active form of vitamin B12) may have similar benefits too!

A Plant-Based Diet can be an excellent way for athletes to improve their performance. With plenty of energy-boosting nutrients, athletes can easily power up their workouts and achieve fitness goals. Give it a try today!

CHAPTER TWELVE: HOW TO EAT TO LOSE WEIGHT BUT NOT YOUR MUSCLE

They say that dieting is the surest way to lose weight. For most people, it's true, especially if you pick a carefully planned out diet where you eat a lot of nutritious foods. How about those looking to lose weight fast? And want to keep their muscle and not waste it away? Well then, these tips are just for you. We all want to lose weight, but we don't always want to do it in a way that compromises our health. The good news is that you can lose weight without

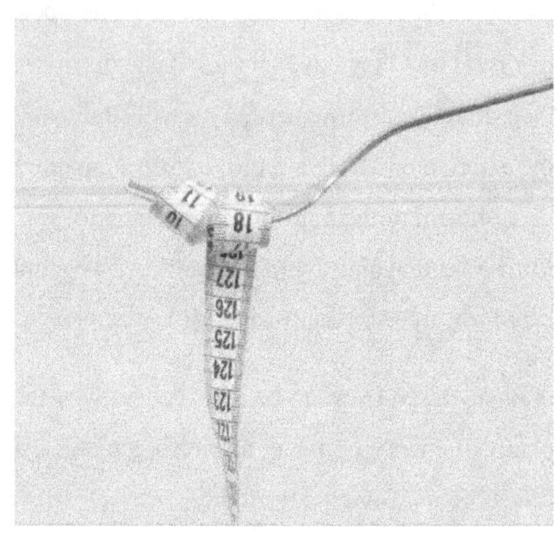

losing muscle while on a plant-based diet. Plant-based diets are typically high in fiber, antioxidants, and phytonutrients and low in saturated fat and cholesterol. There are many benefits to following a plant-based diet, including weight loss, reduced risk of heart disease, cancer, other chronic diseases, and improved energy levels.

I.   Focus on quality, not quantity.

If you want to lose weight, know that quality is just as important as quantity when it comes to food. When creating meals derived from plant-based sources, wholesome fruits and vegetables are a much more valuable source of essential nutrients like fiber and vitamins and help keep you satisfied longer than a bag of potato chips or a box of cookies. Plus, snacking on other plant-based foods like beans and chickpeas can add some extra flavor to your food and help fill in for items that might be missing in your diet - all without costing you any extra calories!

II.   Include protein in every meal.

Protein is essential for maintaining muscle mass, so make sure you get enough of it every day. Include protein in each meal, and consider adding a plant-based protein powder to your smoothies for an extra boost. Researchers suggest eating 25-35% of your calories as protein to maximize fat loss. If you consume 2000 calories per day, 30% of your calories amount to 150g of protein.

- **Protein reduces the level of the hunger hormone**.

Protein naturally helps people lose weight by reducing their levels of the hunger hormone ghrelin while boosting their levels of appetite-reducing hormones GLP-1, peptide YY, and cholecystokinin. This leads to an automatic reduction in calorie intake, improves satiety, and increases fat loss.

- **Protein burns your calories during digestion and metabolism.**

Protein can help with weight loss in two ways. Firstly, during digestion, your body burns calories breaking down, digesting, and metabolizing that protein. And secondly, after you eat, some of the food you consume might be burned by working off the calories from the food or 'thermic effect' as we like to call it! That's 20-30% of protein calories burned from TEF (thermic effect).

- **Protein Increases your "Calories Out"**

Protein is an essential building block for the health and fitness industry. Everyone interested in getting their body into the best shape possible strives to follow a diet high in protein content. The correct ratio of protein to carbohydrate and fats is crucial for losing weight, but more importantly, building lean mass. A high protein intake boosts metabolism and increases the number of calories burned by about 80-100 per day. There are several other factors, but due to the high thermogenic effect that protein has, any diet involving a large number of proteins will help you achieve your goals without much effort.

But remember overfeeding will spoil everything you've achieved and even increase your calories by as much as 260 per day, so don't overfeed!

- **Proteins can reduce your appetite too.**

Protein is a great diet choice for those looking to lose weight. High protein diets are a highly effective way to restrict calories and, in turn, achieve weight loss. Protein is also known for causing you to feel fuller for longer, making it much easier to stick to your diet and control yourself when something tempting comes along in front of you.

- **Proteins can reduce your late-night cravings.**

Losing weight is never easy; however, it can be manageable with the proper diet and exercise. Unfortunately, many people who want to lose weight tend to snack at night after having heavy meals during the day. This destroys any progress you have made throughout the day because instead of burning off your energy, it gets turned into excess fat. How do you fight this? Through protein! Eating more protein can significantly reduce cravings as well as nighttime snacking. Reducing these cravings and sleep-time snacking will make following a healthy diet much easier and more sustainable in the long run for anyone serious about losing weight.

What do you eat to get enough protein? The best way to get a good amount of protein into your diet is through animal sources such as meat, poultry, fish, eggs, and dairy. But that's not the only way. Other good sources of protein are plant-based foods such as Legumes. Lentils, beans, peas, edamame/soybeans (and products made from soy: tofu, tempeh, etc.), and peanuts are delicious and nutritious legumes packed with protein, making them an essential part of any plant-based diet. Whole grains such as Kamut, Teff, Wheat, Quinoa, Rice, Wild Rice, Millet, Oats, and Buckwheat have you covered! A nutritious and protein-packed snack option, nuts and seeds like almonds, cashews, and walnuts are a great way to fuel your body. Hazelnuts, pecans, hemp seeds, pumpkin seeds, sunflower seeds, flax seeds, sesame seeds, and chia seeds are excellent protein sources. Corn, broccoli, asparagus, brussels sprouts, and artichokes are some examples of vegetables and fruits that contain higher protein levels than other plant-based foods.

III. Be mindful of carbohydrates in your diet.

A general rule of thumb to reduce carbs is to eat less bread, rice, pasta, flour, and anything with simple carbohydrates. Simple carbohydrates are usually the most popular choice and easy to digest, passing through the system and being converted into glucose (stored as fat) faster than complex carbs. Simple carbs also give you more energy almost immediately, meaning that if you eat a meal of simple carbohydrates, you could get sluggish at some point and be tempted to have another high-carb snack that could push your calorie count well over your daily limit! The faster the simple, complex carbohydrates break down, the quicker you'll gain weight. That's why complex carbohydrates are recommended for those looking to lose weight. They give you time to hit the gym before getting fat from said carbs. Try to eat more vegetables, fruits, nuts, and seeds. These are low in carbs, and you can eat unlimited amounts!

On a plant-based diet, your primary source of protein should be from plant sources. These include legumes, nuts, and seeds. These foods also contain high amounts of fiber. There are many healthy high, protein, plant-based foods that you can eat to help you lose weight. Eating fewer carbs and more protein can help you lose weight. However, it is still important to exercise and consume fewer overall calories.

Simple carbs generally have a high glycemic index. Glycemic load is the number of carbs from a particular food per gram of that food. It's a measurement of how quickly carbs get digested by your body. This is why we don't want to overindulge in foods with a high glycemic index because the faster carbs are digested, the higher the insulin levels, leading to weight gain. Some plant-based foods with a low glycemic index (55 and below) include fruits such as Apples, Oranges, Dates, and Bananas. Whole grains low in GI are Multigrain bread, Barley, Sweet corn, and Whole-wheat spaghetti. Vegetables in this category can include Cabbage, Broccoli, Onions, and Lettuce. Pulses in this category are Lentils, Kidney beans, Soya beans, and Chickpeas.

Carbs should provide 45–65% of your daily calorie intake for all age groups and sexes. According to the Food and Drug Administration, a recommended daily intake on a 2,000-calorie diet would be 300 grams per day. Some people, however, have decided to reduce their daily carb intake to lose weight. This has been known to go down as low as 50–150 grams per day, depending on eating.

IV.   Eat foods high in fiber.

High-fiber foods are very good at making people feel fuller for more extended periods. This is why people who want to lose weight are encouraged to eat more high-fiber foods. There are two types of fiber: soluble and insoluble. Fiber is a type of carbohydrate that the body does not digest but absorbs and uses. Soluble fiber dissolves in water and beans, broccoli, and apples. Insoluble fiber does not dissolve in water and can be found in wheat bran, nuts, seeds, and whole grains. Research shows that a higher dietary fiber intake is linked to lower weight and overall health. Therefore, eating more high-fiber foods like vegetables, fruits, and whole grains can significantly affect weight loss.

V.   Eat more often!

I know you've heard this before, but eating six small meals throughout the day can be beneficial when trying to lose weight. Eating smaller portions more frequently helps prevent you from overeating, and it keeps your metabolism elevated.

VI.   Make exercise a priority!

I know this is easier said than done sometimes, but if you want results, you have to put in the work at the gym. When you are working out, make sure that you push yourself as hard as possible because that's what will lead to the most results. Fitness is an integral part of losing weight. It would be best if you made exercise a priority in your life. Set an appointment with yourself to go to the gym or exercise outside for about 30 minutes every day. The key is consistency. If you don't make a habit of exercising, chances are you'll give up before you start to lose weight. It can be challenging to exercise regularly. It's an uphill battle, and you have to have a routine that you stick with.

The more often you exercise, the easier it is to continue this routine. Losing weight is just the beginning. Focus on how to keep the weight off, and you'll be doing yourself a huge favor! You can also try other workouts like swimming, cycling, jogging, yoga, dancing. The list is endless; just do the exercise that you love most.

VII.   Drink lots of water!

Losing weight is not easy. Staying motivated and setting goals can be a huge challenge at times. One of the best ways to realize your weight loss goals is to drink lots of water. Drinking water can help you feel full more quickly and keep you from being dehydrated. Dehydration can lead to poor sleep habits and poor digestion. By staying hydrated, you can make sure your body is in the best possible shape to lose weight and keep it off! Drink that water! Aim to drink at least half your body weight (in ounces) each day. For example, if you weigh 150 lbs., aim for 75 ounces of water per day.

VIII.   Acknowledging that it's ok to have a cheat day

To lose weight and keep it off, you have to be a healthy person's mindset. That means sometimes accepting that you could allow yourself to cheat on your diet. If you don't enjoy the things you eat or make yourself miserable, then your diet won't work correctly.

That's why it's essential to make sure you enjoy the foods you eat and that you don't feel like you're depriving yourself of anything. Of course, you'll want to make sure you avoid any foods that could be fattening in high amounts. Either way, cheat days are essential to have in the process of losing weight, but you have to be reasonable about it. Don't eat so much that you spoil your diet for the rest of the week!

IX.   Get enough sleep

Getting enough sleep is essential to losing weight and maintaining weight loss. Sleep is when your body is recovering from the stresses of the day. If you don't get enough rest, your metabolism can slow down, your appetite can increase, and your immune system weakens. The key to losing weight and maintaining your weight loss is to find a healthy balance between the amount of sleep you need and the amount of sleep you get. If you're already getting enough sleep and still want to lose weight, you can try cutting off your snacking earlier in the day and making sure you get your exercise every day!

X.   Focus on whole foods

The thought of losing weight might seem overwhelming, but a great way to start is by focusing on whole foods.

By eating whole foods, you're not only cutting out processed and fast foods, which can be great for losing weight, but you're also eating more vegetables! Make sure you're eating a range of vegetables every day, and you'll feel your diet improving significantly, and thus your weight loss. Try one new vegetable every week to expand your palate and your waistline!

XI.   Try not to skip meals.

If weight loss is one of your goals, you might be pursuing it through a plant-based diet, and remember that you should not skip meals. As the saying goes, you need to eat breakfast like a king, lunch like a prince, and dinner like a pauper if you want to burn fat. The benefits of restricting animal products alone are enough, but the fact that plant-based foods provide fewer calories than traditional American dishes can help to accelerate your weight loss! If you're trying to lose weight fast, skipping meals might seem like a quick solution. However, the reality is that you're going to need the nutrition from foods as well as regular exercise to keep yourself healthy and happy. Besides, fiber-rich vegetable meals will help keep you full for longer, so you won't have room for unhealthy snacking between meals and also late at night. Starving yourself is not part of the plant-based diet; focus on healthy meal preparation and give your body the food it needs to be active and healthy.

XII.   Cut your intake of oils.

Losing weight on a plant-based diet can be very simple. Eating a plant-based diet is about consuming the right food in the right quantities. By keeping track of what you eat, you can ensure that fat is not a part of your daily nutrition. While many fats in the world are essential to a healthy diet, consuming too much can cause weight gain. Many people are entirely unaware of how much oil they consume throughout the day! If you're interested in losing weight on a plant-based diet, make sure you're not eating foods that are high in unhealthy fats. Some nuts and seeds, like macadamia nuts, cashews, pistachios, almonds, walnuts, and sesame seeds, are naturally very high in the polyunsaturated omega-3 ALA, which are the good fats that you can consume. Saturated fats and trans fats have been linked to contributing to weight gain. Bacon, sausage, red meat, cookies, chips, crackers, and fries are examples of foods that contain saturated and trans fats. It's best to exercise in moderation and not eat these foods every day or even every week.

XIII.   Don't give up just yet.

It's natural to be upset if you don't see weight loss results as you would like. While every diet is different, we know that you're focusing on eating whole foods and mostly plants with a plant-based diet, which will be a healthier alternative to refined, processed foods. Most people who switch to a plant-based diet meal plan for weight loss want to see results within weeks, but occasionally results aren't as dramatic as dieters hope. If you've committed to the diet and you still aren't losing as much weight as you want, give your body some time to adjust and make sure you're following the plan correctly. If you're not seeing results after several weeks or months, your body might not be responding to the diet as well as you'd like. It is possible to switch to a vegan diet for weight loss, but it might not be the best for you. You can switch to other plant-based diets to experiment with what works for you. If you're healthy and trying to drop a few pounds, it can take up to 4 weeks to lose 1-2 pounds. If you're overweight and need to lose 100 lbs, you will see quicker results.

So there you have it! Follow these tips, and you can lose weight without losing muscle while on a plant-based diet. Just remember to be patient and stay consistent, and before you know it, you'll be seeing the results you've been working so hard for. Good luck!

CHAPTER THIRTEEN: HOW A PLANT-BASED DIET CAN IMPROVE YOUR SEX LIFE

Plant-Based Diet Can Boost Your Sex Drive And Your Performance In Bed!

We've all heard that a healthy diet is essential for improving our health and wellbeing. Plant-based diets are typically high in fiber, antioxidants, and phytonutrients and low in saturated fat and cholesterol. There are many benefits to following a plant-based diet, including weight loss, reduced risk of heart disease, cancer, and other chronic diseases, improved energy levels, and easier maintenance of a healthy weight. While these are all great things for your overall wellbeing, did you know that they can also affect your sex life?

Sex is lovely; it's a part of life we should all embrace. Unfortunately, many factors are at play when satisfying your partner and how frequently you have them. Plant-based diets have been shown to boost testosterone, which increases libido, sexual function and overall sex drive. Vegan and vegetarian diets are also natural diuretics, meaning that you are more likely to feel more at the moment as you will be less likely to experience erectile dysfunction. It's all about the nutrients you're consuming and what they do to help your body function properly. For example, if you are deficient in B12, that can cause problems with arousal and fertility. And when it comes to hormones, low estrogen levels can lead to vaginal dryness, which is uncomfortable at best and painful at worst. But there is hope! There are simple things to incorporate into your life to help you have better sex: eat a more plant-based diet, exercise regularly, and have a more positive outlook on your sex life. A great way to start your day is with breakfast, such as beans, tofu scramble, or lentil soup. Yes. Please.

According to some studies, a plant-based diet can enhance a man's sexual life. The increased energy levels of vegans have been linked to improved libido. The consumption of plants also helps the penis and organs function properly. This makes the body healthier and more responsive to sex. Therefore, a plant-based diet can boost a man's sex life.

A. A Plant-Based Diet Plant-based Can Bring Relief If You're Suffering from Erectile Dysfunction

Studies have shown that a plant-based diet can improve a man's sexual life. According to Aaron Spitz, a urologist, a plant-based diet can cure erectile dysfunction permanently. In the documentary The Game Changers, he performed a study that showed that men on a vegan diet had a higher frequency and harder erections. The findings can be a lifelong relief to many men suffering from this condition.

B. A Plant-Based Diet Offers Better Lubrication For Women

Eating plant-based diets can help you have a better sex life. Hydrating your body is essential for having a healthy and enjoyable sex life, especially for women. Plant-based foods are very high in water content, giving women more vaginal lubrication naturally. The good news is many vegan foods are super hydrating such as watermelon, cucumbers, green leafy vegetables, berries, among others. The high water content also 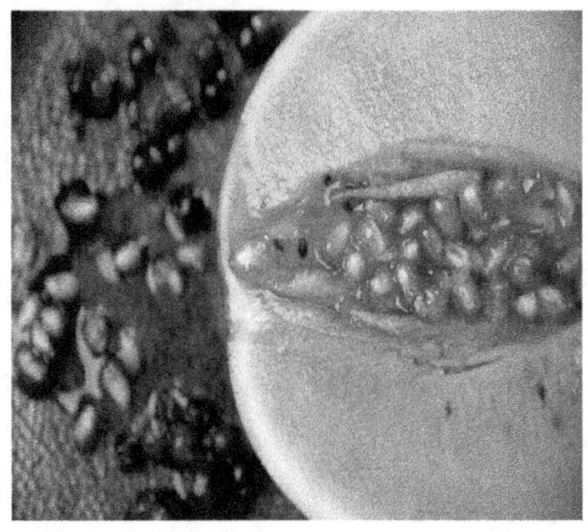 contributes to having better skin and reducing the number of wrinkles you have, and lessening dryness in your body.

C. A Plant-Based Diet improves your Blood Flow and Overall Health, For Women Too.

Eating a plant-based diet can improve your sex life by improving your overall health. It can reverse fatty deposits in arteries and improve blood flow, increasing libido and sex performance. Additionally, plant-based diets are rich in fiber, vitamins, and minerals. If you want to have a better sex life, a plant-based diet can give you a better flow and make you rise to the occasion.

D. A Plant-Based Diet puts You in the Mood To Make Love.

A plant-based diet can have surprising benefits. It increases the amount of serotonin, which is linked to oxytocin, the love hormone responsible for feelings of affection and intimacy. Oxytocin is sometimes called the 'love' hormone, making vegans want to get closer with their partners beyond physical intimacy. Oxytocin is responsible for all those cuddles you wish to after making love, so even after you've exerted your energy with one another, you're still more inclined to cuddle and snuggle. This is an excellent first step.

E. A Plant-Based Diet Improves Your Libido

Sometimes, it can be challenging to get back into the romantic groove, especially for those working on a busy schedule, but if you know that your diet is helping you out in more ways than one, you'll be less likely to lose hope. According to several psychology studies, couples who eat together have better communication within their relationship. Three foods found to help increase libido include bananas, avocados & chickpeas. Other foods include leafy greens, almonds, pumpkin seeds, dark chocolate, and cayenne pepper. These are all common vegan foods rich in zinc and B vitamins. You can get some of these vitamins from other foods such as fish, but once you're on a plant-based diet, these foods form part of daily diets as well, which should come as no surprise! We're sure everyone is aware of the phrase; food is love, and if you know what causes your partner to be more inclined towards loving you back, wouldn't you try it? A plant-based diet has been proven to improve the libido of both men and women.

Compared to non-vegetarians, vegans have lower levels of fatty acids in their bodies, responsible for enhancing sex performance. Some studies also found that vegans have lower blood pressure. Moreover, they were more likely to have a higher libido than non-vegetarians.

F. A Plant-Based Diet Improves Your Stamina

You're probably excited to see what eating a plant-based diet has been doing for your health in general, but maybe you're surprised at how much more energy you've been having! Eating nuts, fresh fruit, and fresh vegetables will always result in eating healthier and feeling better. The great thing about eating vegan is that it's impossible to get over-stuffed from consuming way too much sugar (unless you decide to have cake, I don't have any problems with a vegan cake). Plant-based enthusiasts like Vegans worldwide report their libidos increasing with their energy as a whole! This can be great for your sex life.

A plant-based diet can also increase the amount of sex-enhancing antioxidants in the body. It also boosts libido and improves the overall health of a man. Those who are overweight and have diabetes may want to eat a plant-based diet. It can improve their overall physical and emotional wellbeing. While a plant-based diet may not enhance your libido, it can reduce the risk of cardiovascular disease.

G. A Plant-based diet Makes You Smell Better.

A plant-based diet can help you smell better, which can help improve your sex life. The science is simple: people who eat meat and dairy have higher levels of steroids, resulting in an odor similar to sweat, which is considered unattractive when mating. On the other hand, plant-based diets include vegetables and fruit, including all other plant-based foods like grains, legumes and nuts. A plant-based diet also includes fewer animal products and less processed foods. These foods don't give off too much body odor; vegans have more alluring natural scents. The smell of most people's sweat is not something others enjoy being around. With a plant-based diet, this smell is reduced. This can allow for more enjoyable personal interactions.

H. Having a Healthy Weight Is Good For Better Sex

Consistently packing in extra weight can make you lazy in the bedroom. Obesity can often lead to low libido and a lower sex drive. It's not uncommon for obesity to cause genital issues, infertility, and more commonly associated with hormonal imbalances. A healthy lifestyle that focuses on eating less processed foods could help eliminate your unwanted pounds—which will improve your sex life. You'll have more incredible stamina for longer and be free to experiment with new positions, thanks to the fact that you'll be able to squat and spread your legs with ease!

I. A Plant-Based Diet Will Make You Look Better

Plant-Based Diets such as Vegan diets will not only make you happier, but they have been

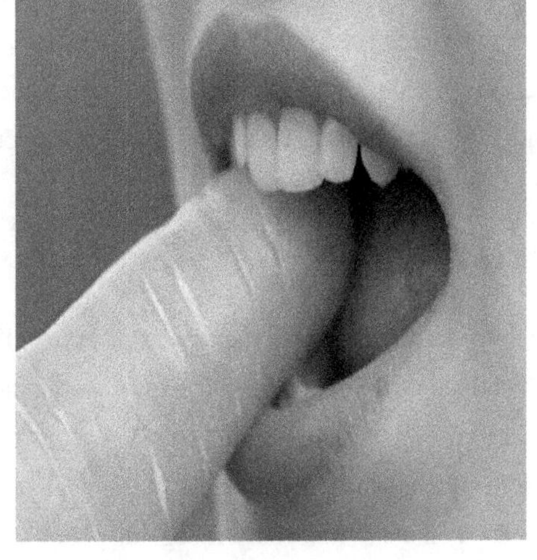

known to both improve and maintain a body's overall health. This is great, especially if your partner happens to be vegan too. The increased intake of vitamin C that dieters see can produce an abundance of benefits. Firstly, it means that your skin will look and feel healthier! You'll notice that your skin will become silkier, softer and smoother all around.

Additionally, many people who adopt a vegan diet report experiencing their best skin in over ten years! This has to do with the antioxidants that fill the fruits and vegetables we eat daily when following a vegan diet. Feeling better and attractive to your partner can spice up things between the sheets – just one more reason why those thinking about adopting one should take action sooner rather than later!

Some Plant-Based Foods to get you in the mood.

- **Soy**

A lot of women experience a decline in their sex drive during menopause. This is unfortunate because there are ways to combat low estrogen levels and still feel your most orgasms.

Right now, you may be asking, "what can I do about it!?" Well, we're happy to report that one of the best foods for this purpose is soy, which contains phytoestrogens that can boost lower levels of estrogen and libido by mimicking or replacing the hormone in the body!

- **Avocados**

Are you looking to spice up your sex life? Try putting some avocado on your sandwiches; they're packed with Vitamin B6 - which can reduce premenstrual symptoms like bloating, fatigue and irritability. This, in turn, will make you more attractive to members of the opposite nookie!

- **Quinoa**

Would you rather have an increased sex drive or the energy to stay awake all night? Well, one way to do both is by adding quinoa to your diet for breakfast! This delicious grain is packed with protein that could be the key to boosting testosterone. Not only will it help you have more stamina in bed, but it'll also assist in regulating hormone levels and improving libido. You might find yourself begging your guy to get some rest while you "sweep" him away...

- **Almonds**

Nuts are often packed with protein and healthy fats. Consider having almonds in your diet. They have an abundance of Vitamin E, a nutrient that encourages the production of sex hormones within the body. In doing so, it has been proven that consuming Vitamin E-rich foods like almonds can improve a person's sex life, resulting in longer and more enjoyable intercourse for both parties involved!

- **Watermelon**

Some of us know that the key to better sex life is something as simple as a good night's rest. However, did you know that watermelon can improve your sex life? While having several vitamins and nutrients in it, watermelon has citrulline, which relaxes and dilates blood vessels like Viagra, which some people use to treat erectile dysfunction. Consuming watermelons can positively affect one's sex life, mainly if you include them in your daily diet, thanks to citrulline.

- **Fenugreek**

Herb Fenugreek might increase your libido. It makes a great addition to any homemade curry. Try adding it to your homemade curries with lots of healthy veggies.

- **Basil**

Basil can help many women out there to improve the quality of their sex life. Basil is one herb that has a fantastic effect on the human body. It can act as an aphrodisiac to both men and women. People who have used basil in their dishes or during sexual intercourse say that they can sense themselves being more sensual, alive, and quite simply desiring more.

- **Dark Chocolate**

Recently I bought groceries, and as I started unloading my shopping bag, I couldn't help but notice how much dark chocolate was in there. It turns out that this was all my husband's doing. He said that he had read somewhere that eating it makes you feel good initially because of all the happy hormones it releases (serotonin, endorphins) and that it makes us sexier because serotonin levels can increase someone's libido. Having raised eyebrows and a big grin on my face from hearing this from him, he proceeded to say that we pretty much couldn't go wrong with stocking up on this score - anyway, who is going to deny their partner more sex?

- **Pomegranate**

A daily glass of pomegranate juice can be a great way to spice up your sex life. It's been proven to increase sexual desire, improve mood and blood circulation, and raise testosterone levels. This not only increases libido in women, especially after menopause but also in both men and women.

- **Asparagus**

Chock-full of vitamin E, asparagus is a great choice when you're feeling amorous. The natural herb increases blood and oxygen flow to the genitals, which can help you start having some fun in the bedroom! Asparagus may be low in calories and packed with dietary fiber, but its high concentration of vitamin E will surely get your motor running. And there's no need for any lubrication, so speak freely (if using fronds) about what kinds of things are turning you on.

- **Ginger**

Ginger is a superfood that supports the good circulation of blood. Do you know what else people go for when they want the same effect? The blue pills! Incorporating ginger into your daily diet is probably one of the best decisions you'll ever make because it will help improve the blood flow to your nether regions. This means more chances for enjoying a healthy and fulfilling sex life, whether alone or with a partner. It doesn't hurt if you throw this tasty root into your recipe book either: not just does mixing it with any cuisine add an extra depth of flavor in itself, but the fact that it boosts the body's circulation will also help kick things off in the bedroom too. What are you waiting for? Throw some ginger into your next meal - and get going!

- **Bananas**

Fruit helps a man's love life. Eating bananas gives you stamina in the bedroom. Bananas are popular as they contain magnesium, which increases sexual stamina, and potassium helps improve testosterone hormone in men, affecting a man's sexual behavior.

- **Saffron**

If you're someone who has a hard time getting or staying erect, adding saffron spice to your diet may help. Saffron is a herb used in Ayurveda medicine and other holistic healing practices. It's also been shown that this spice can be used for hair and skin health. Still, it's most well-known for its aphrodisiac properties, with research showing it may help people experience better arousal desire and boost overall sexual function in both males and females. This herb can be on the pricey side compared to others spices, so if your wallet isn't overflowing with cash, you can try growing your own using seedlings that are easy to buy at the local farmers' market!

- **Figs**

If a fig is fresh, it will be moist with bright green flesh, and if it is dried, it will feel lighter than expected for its size with soft and brittle, brown skin. A fresh fig should have ripe stems, which give way halfway down. While all figs are edible, some of them are considered too inconsistent with eating unless you're familiar with their flavor. Strangely enough, the most delicious of these capricious ones are the kinds that are named after women.

Come back to your bedroom for one moment. This fruit is considered the pièce de résistance of seduction because it resembles a female's sexual organs. This scientific find, according to scientists, turns men on. Getting turned on around your partner will spice things up in your bedroom and improve your romantic life.

CHAPTER FOURTEEN: REJUVENATING YOUR BRAIN A PLANT-BASED DIET

It's no question that plant-based foods have some amazing health benefits, such as sustaining a weight loss diet as well as giving you more energy! But what effects does it have on your brain? It's time to find out!

If you have ever met someone who seems to always be in a bad mood, there is a good chance they don't eat well. That kind of diet will keep your brain (and all other major systems) running slow, significantly reducing the person's ability to think clearly. On the other hand, when we feed our bodies healthy plant-based foods, our brains are better able to focus, enjoy life more and stay ahead of the curve.

More and more, health-conscious people are turning to plant-based diets as an alternative to their old eating habits. Many people have experienced the positive effects this switch has brought upon them. Dr. Michael Greger explains how a positive lifestyle change can affect just about everything positively: 'The result is that you're not only treating the cause of these things… you are also improving your cognitive abilities, your moods—and even how well you sleep! Plant-based eating makes it easier to build muscle and lose fat. Experts agree that it helps protect against heart disease and cancer.

The more regularly you opt for a plant-based diet, the more likely it is that your body weight and blood sugar levels will fall into a healthy range and control cholesterol; this is not to mention emotional states. This will also improve your general health by getting rid of "ageing toxins."

These toxins are created in heat-processed foods— hamburgers and hot dogs, chips and crackers, processed cheese —due to the tremendous ratio of free radicals or damaging oxygen radicals produced. In addition to this, glycotoxins have been linked to diabetes and cardiovascular disease.

Does a Plant-Based Diet Offer Long-Term Benefits on your Brain Health?

The Mediterranean diet is an excellent example of how eating plant-based foods can have positive long-term effects on your health. This diet, popular in Mediterranean countries, consists of consuming many vegetarian foods and very little meat. Studies show that people who live where the diet is commonplace are generally healthier and live longer than those who don't follow the same trend, making them less likely to fall victim to chronic illnesses like heart disease and cancer.

A plant-based diet that excludes nitrates and nitrites also avoids the harm that these preservatives can potentially cause. These unwanted preservatives have been suggested to increase the risks of dementia, which is why a team from the University of Pittsburgh Medical Center surveyed fish-eating vegetarians and vegans who didn't eat meat but did consume fish. When compared with omnivores and pescetarians, they experienced less risk in terms of memory loss over time as predicted.

Are Omega-3 Fatty Acids and Vitamin B12 Important For Your Brain Health?

Going Plant-Based, such as Veganism, doesn't just mean being against consuming meats and animal products; it also means being against the torture of animals in general. This may be a noble cause, but sadly, it might also bring some unfavorable consequences. Your mind may be one of them if you do not consider putting in some effort to acquire certain nutrients that you would otherwise consume via meat and dairy products. These crucial nutrients are known by many names, including B12 vitamins and fish oil fatty acids, which play an essential role in maintaining a healthy brain.

Vitamin B12 is the powerhouse in your cells, helping to create DNA and red blood cells. This vitamin isn't naturally produced within the body, so you must get enough of it each day!

So how can you ensure this happens? One way is to drink plenty of dairy products or take Vitamin B12 supplements to help reach adequate intake levels. You may not think that fish have any relevance to your diet. Still, they offer an incredibly high amount of Omega-3 fatty acids, which are crucial for a well-functioning body and reducing inflammation! Sometimes these amazing nutrients are found in seafood such as crayfish and salmon - or take supplements to get more of them.

Eating your fruit and vegetables does help to keep you cleaner from the inside out. That being said, it's essential not to forget about cleaning your brain! You see, this muscle is incredibly complex, and it needs a lot of attention so that it functions at its best. To make sure you meet all of your brain's requirements for optimal performance, take good care of it by eating plenty of brain boosters like leafy greens, lean proteins, fatty fish, nuts, and seeds. A balanced diet might also help prevent Alzheimer's disease or other forms of dementia.

Boost Your Brain With These Plant-Based Food Sources

- **Foods rich in Antioxidants**

The brain requires a lot of energy. We use it to solve new problems, to learn new skills, and of course, we sometimes use it for sitting and resting. You and I may have our brain preservation secrets, but there is one fact that scientists have determined about the structure of the brain: how we keep our brains healthy has a crucial impact on whether or not we live to see that next birthday.

The brain is vulnerable to oxidative damage, which is essentially when cells, proteins, and DNA become damaged by excessive amounts of free radicals. A diet high in antioxidant-rich foods can help protect your precious grey matter. Healthy fruits and vegetables – such as berries, peaches, avocado, asparagus, spinach tomatoes (and tomato products), onions, and garlic – are rich in antioxidants such as glutathione which gets made in the body via the process of methylation. And some veggies are especially good for increasing sulfur levels too! Therefore, all these wonderful plant-based foods make great additions to a diet that helps keep brain cells functioning at their best!

- **Foods rich in Tryptophan**

We all know the feeling of being so comfortably full at dinner that you are ready to take a nap. Tryptophan, an essential amino acid that creates sleep-friendly serotonins to keep you happy and stable during stressful or upsetting times, is commonly found in proteins like turkey. Yet surprisingly enough, it can also be found in many other plant-based sources like nuts, tofu, beans, seeds, oats, and lentils! So as a brain-boosting snack, pick up some of these foods high in tryptophan today!

- **Foods rich in Probiotics**

Like other live yeasts and bacteria, probiotics are found in certain foods, such as sauerkraut and kimchi, as well as in supplements. According to research, these live cultures can help balance the good and bad bacteria in your gut. They also replenish good bacteria, which may have been killed off naturally or by consuming too many antibiotics. Recent studies also show that our enteric nervous system, a nerve network in the gastrointestinal tract that affects our digestion and brain function, creates a "second brain" in our gut. Perhaps you've heard things like this before but never realized how deep it runs? It's essential after learning this information to include more probiotic foods into your diet since they promote better overall health!

- **Leafy greens**

Spinach, kale, and Swiss chard are not just green leafy vegetables that we pop in our mouths. They are power-packed plants loaded with nutrients mainly targeted at the brain. Both folate and Vitamin K are essential for excellent memory and cognitive skill, while beta carotene gives energy to your brain so that you can achieve peak productivity. Just one serving of raw spinach contains 121 percent of the daily value of Vitamin K, which means you get a lot more than 100% as what's recommended on the label. You get all this while taking in no cholesterol or sodium - two main villains in compromising cognitive ability. Chuck all three of these into a salad or smoothie for a complete brain food meal!

- **Seeds**

Seeds are tiny but mighty! Chia, flax, and hemp seeds are high in essential fatty acids, which can help to reduce the onset of cognitive decline. Omega-3 is getting some serious recognition these days - it's been linked to lowering your risk of cancer and heart disease, improving joint health, and helping with weight loss and digestion. You already know that omega-3 fatty acids are good for your heart, but they've been shown not to harm healthy blood vessels while lowering insulin resistance. Think of them as the crutch looking out for your circulatory system! And that's far from all they're capable of. Think about all the ways you can get the most out of this amazing seed by adding it to roasted vegetables or even just a bit sprinkled on top of a dish like oatmeal, salads, or even soups.

- **Spices**

People have been using various herbs for medicinal purposes for hundreds of years, and in recent decades, their validity has received more attention. This is primarily due to their antioxidant and anti-inflammatory properties, which help improve brain function. Turmeric, saffron, cinnamon, pepper, and rosemary are just some examples of spices that have been proven to help enhance your memory. Many people swear by the power of curcumin found in spice turmeric to cope with anxiety-related issues such as ADD/ADHD or simply stay alert while driving long distances. Women often use turmeric specifically when they are pregnant because it is a healthy way to prevent morning sickness without taking medications or altering their daily routines too much. These spices are also fat-free, sodium-free, and completely natural, so they can still feel as if they're indulging in a good meal even while they're trying to eat healthier!

- **Dark Chocolate**

Good for you? Chocolate has flavonols and antioxidants that have anti-inflammatory qualities and improve cognitive functioning. The dark stuff contains more "good" nutrients than milk chocolate or white chocolate. To get the healthiest dose of brain food possible, settle on treats with a cocoa content of 80 percent or higher. Non-processed cocoa means a greater chance of enjoying cocoa's purported health benefits.

Now, sneak spoonfuls -- just a few! -- into your hot chocolate to make it even healthier with an extra dose of antioxidants, or add a square to your yogurt when sweetening it up. And if you're planning on devouring the whole bar, well, no favors will be granted!

- **Berries**

The next time you want a delicious, healthy snack, pop one of these power-packed fruits into your mouth! Strawberries, blueberries, and raspberries are high in antioxidants and fiber, both of which can make you feel energized—sometimes called anti-aging berries (yep, they're that good for you) because they act as cleansers in the body. These little berry treats also contain polyphenols to fight inflammation in the brain. No better way to keep your brain on task!

- **Soy**

Soy products have been linked to improved cognitive function, like brainpower. When soybeans are eaten, they get converted into isoflavones that act as the human hormone estrogen. Yogurt that contains this natural ingredient has also been noted for its mental health benefits. Soybeans contain a beneficial vitamin known as B-complex. Some people say it helps regulate weight loss, another reason so many states in East Asia embrace tofu-heavy diets to fight obesity! A single serving of tofu contains 0.4 mg of thiamine, equating to 33 percent of your recommended daily intake. If you want to ensure you stay healthy while taking advantage of this fantastic food source, you can consume it in many forms by choosing from various soy foods like soybeans, miso, tempeh (fermented tofu), and soy sauce. However, beware of processed soy that has been produced using chemicals or pesticides because this kind is harmful to your health.

- **Complex Carbohydrates**

Complex carbohydrates are turned into glucose in the body, like fuel for our brain. Like a motor without any gas, we have no energy to analyze or process information effectively; hence, making us feel sluggish and almost dragging us down! However, they don't impact our insulin levels as simple carbohydrates. One serving of either oat bran, wheat bran, and lima beans can provide over 50 percent of our recommended daily fiber intake. As stated before, brain function relies on glucose to properly function and can be severely affected by low levels.

Therefore it's up to us to supply the body with glucose from food sources like complex carbs so that our brain can do what it does best! Add fiber-rich foods to your meals, which will leave you feeling super energized and satiated. You are what you eat. Incorporating a plant-based diet full of these brain foods can improve mental tasks, such as alertness, concentration, and memory.

CHAPTER FIFTEEN: PLANT-BASED LIFESTYLE AND MENTAL HEALTH

Can Plant Foods Fight Your Moods?

Lots of people become depressed and can't accomplish the simplest of tasks. Sometimes that's

because they're burnt out from working hard every day. When this happens, we encourage you to take a break every day from work, not to burn yourself out because we know it's challenging and crucial to maintaining balance in one's life. If you can't manage that, try changing your diet to avoid getting too hungry or distracted. We all know how easily these things happen because everyone is busy rushing around and trying so hard to prove themselves in today's ever-growing market.

Diet has a significant effect on one's mood and mental health. Foods with high sugar content are, in fact, neurotoxic to one's brain and unfortunately even lead to more anxiety, bad temper, and lack of concentration, so avoiding them (or curtailing their consumption) can lessen or eliminate anxiety and depression over time. Animal-based products contain pro-inflammatory compounds such as arachidonic acid that can have a negative effect on depression and the risk of suicide.

Have you heard of it? Eating a plant-based diet can help improve depression, anxiety, and brain fog. Not to mention, it can help decrease your risk for diabetes, high blood pressure, heart disease, stroke, colorectal diseases, and many other chronic illnesses. A whole, intact plant foods are full of fibers, vitamins, and minerals, while animal-based products are deficient in the same mood-regulating nutrients.

Inflammation and imbalanced neurotransmitters have explicitly been linked to depression. However, scientists have found that healthy plant foods, in general, may help to decrease brain inflammation and cellular damage. Researchers have also confirmed that plant foods high in antioxidants (phytochemicals) can help alleviate depression by stopping the buildup of damaging compounds and restoring balance to one's neurotransmitter levels. Many individuals suffering from major depressive disorder (MDD) usually have elevated levels of an enzyme called monoamine oxidase or MOA. This is because it plays a significant role in regulating serotonin levels and other essential brain chemicals (i.e., dopamine).

Ingesting certain sub-categories or specific types of fruits and vegetables should help you lower MAO levels and maintain healthy serotonin amounts so you can avoid feeling depressed again.

Have you ever heard of eating apples to get rid of sadness? The thing about eating apples is that it makes you feel good because it has quercetin. This can be a natural antidepressant, meaning more serotonin and dopamine will be produced within your brain. Quercetin is a fantastic antioxidant that happens to help fight depression by improving brain health. A person with high levels of this nutrient in their system will feel less stressed out and find themselves much more alert! Foods that contain quercetin include apples, kale, berries, grapes, onions, green tea, and more!

Arachidonic acid serves as a precursor to inflammatory chemicals in our bodies, and it's a type of fat found only in animals. If you eat foods high in this acid, such as eggs and chicken, you set off a cascade of chemical reactions in your body. When inflammation reaches your brain, feelings of anxiety, stress, and depression arise. Interestingly, individuals who avoid foods high in arachidonic acid tend to report a happier and more positive mood. Why does this happen, you might ask? Because when the body is not attacked by inflammation - it simply does not have any reason to attack itself. Just like how the human body responds when exposed to sunlight - we begin to feel energized and cleansed from the inside out. Eliminating inflammatory animal foods from the diet ensures not only physical health but mental health as well!

But Some Researchers Say Grass Ain't Always Greener When You Go Plant-Based!

Not all plant-based diets are healthy - and if one decides on a very low-quality plant-based diet, several side effects could affect us. Some consequences of having a poor diet can include mental fatigue and stress, but the good news is we know how to boost your mental health by practicing a proper diet. Some research has found that a high intake of fruit, vegetables, nuts, and seeds can protect you against mental disorders such as depression. It's widely known, for instance, that those with diets high in fresh produce are at lower risk for depression compared to peers who don't eat as many fruits and veggies. So make sure you're getting enough vitamins from natural sources if you want to prevent yourself from experiencing less than happy feelings when it comes to taking care of yourself!

While research suggests that a high-quality plant-based diet may be an effective way for those suffering from depression to manage their symptoms, it's currently unclear if switching over to a high-quality plant-based diet will lead to immediate relief from symptoms of depression. This concern is due to the possible changes in hormones, stress levels, and eating habits, but I can confidently say that moving towards a healthier lifestyle is always a good thing! But it doesn't necessarily mean swapping your pills is a cure-all.

Someone once told me jokingly that he kills animals because they eat our food (vegans food). Funny and also not funny enough! Vegans and vegetarians have traditionally been classed as strange, and they could potentially suffer from depression more than the overall population. This might be because vegans and vegetarians tend to be very conscious about animal welfare and environmental concerns that not everyone is aware of, making them stick out among many other people and groups who do not have the same beliefs.

Include The Following Plant-Based Foods For a Better Mood

Planning meals can be a tedious task. However, many people fall into a bit of a habit regarding this process. Many people tend to enjoy the comfort of the familiar — and that is alright!

However, if one only eats plate after plate of the same thing every week without mixing it up once in a while, you may not be taking advantage of all that your body has to offer. Don't let yourself get into a rut because you're overeating the same meal! I encourage everyone planning meals to try out different recipes from time to time so you can get as much nutrition as possible for your body. To learn more about how you can stand up for your health in new ways by simply switching up what's on your plate, read on below:

- **Omega-3 Fatty Acids**

Avoid fish for omega 3's; go nuts (literally)! In a study by the University of Pittsburgh, it was found that people with lower levels of marine omega-3 fatty acids tended to have more symptoms of depression. However, they didn't find a similar pattern when comparing plant-based ALA sources or non causally related sources such as purine-rich foods. To be safe, monitor your ALA consumption and keep track of any adverse side effects. Make sure you eat sufficient amounts of walnuts and chia seeds every day. These types of food also happen to be excellent sources of nutrients such as protein, antioxidants, calcium, and fiber, which are great for your well-being whether needed due to a mental illness or not.

- **Tryptophan**

Our modern, busy lives can often lead us to skip meals or grab something unhealthy when short on time. However, skipping meals isn't the answer as it drives our brain to send hunger signals, encouraging us to eat whenever the next opportunity arises. This can cause worries about weight loss and overload your mind with other life concerns, but luckily there are ways to help the relief. One of these ways is using another amino acid to help ease some of your worries. Did you know that your brain uses tryptophan to produce serotonin, the happy neurotransmitter? It's mostly in animal foods such as chicken, fish, and eggs, though the body can have difficulty converting tryptophan to serotonin, you can also get tryptophan from plant-based foods such as leafy greens like spinach and kale, quinoa, mushrooms, broccoli, chickpeas, soybeans, pumpkin seeds, and hummus made from garbanzo beans; sunflower seeds.

- **B Vitamins**

B vitamins are beneficial for keeping one's mind relaxed, calm, and collected during stressful situations. The B vitamins can help one get rid of exhaustion, depression, irritability, etc. These B vitamins are essential in our diet because they are directly related to storing energy in our bodies for later use. Avoiding stress is more helpful than taking medication for it, and a sure way one can avoid stress is by eating foods that have these B vitamins. Eating foods such as beans and lentils, fortified cereals, and sunflower seeds are all great ways to get vitamins and minerals that increase neurotransmitters in our brains. When our brain has the nutrients it needs, we tend to be happier people!

Things To Keep In Mind To Improve Your Mental Health When You Go Plant-Based.

1. Embrace The Process

If you're new to eating plant-based, don't beat yourself up if it takes you a bit of time to grasp the concept of how easy (and dare we say enjoyable!) It is to prepare meals from plants! Think about starting with Meatless Mondays at home and making more homemade meals centered on whole plant foods that appeal to your taste buds. The journey can be stimulating rather than overwhelming. Remember that committing to an animal-free lifestyle requires patience rather than stressing yourself out when things don't go your way. You'll attract mostly positive people into your life, and they'll show you the way with their enlightening knowledge on new products and services available in the marketplace. When you're flying through smooth air, no one minds when they have to endure a bit of turbulence.

2. Plan Ahead

When you go plant-based, you may feel uncomfortable relying on the food choices provided by your environment. You may find it difficult to ensure that what you choose to eat adheres to your dietary requirements in specific social settings or at work. This can lead to you developing unhealthy habits, which may cause weight gain and reduce energy levels.

To remain focused and avoid wasting time looking for meal options while away from home, make sure that you plan out meals and snacks before leaving the house. Bring healthy snack food or a ready-made meal with you in your bag; there is no need to compromise on your daily plant-based intake! Try to set realistic goals for yourself. Track them if you want until they become second nature. Be proud of any progress you make to encourage yourself and others around you!

3. Be Patient

When you first start on a plant-based diet, it can be pretty tricky to start building the good habits of eating whole, plant-based foods. It's essential to try new things and get creative with meals (rather than focusing purely on salads and smoothie bowls) - but it can take some time until your brain starts to let go of those all-too-tempting comfort foods like cheese!

Because our brains become used to certain foods over time, you may feel tempted now and again when you're out at a restaurant or around friends who are eating something similar. But once you've trained your brain to want nutrient-rich veg, fruit, and grains instead of cheeseburgers and chocolate cake - remember, don't beat yourself up. Find alternative options like hiking in the park that can help elevate your mood hormones instead.

4. Find Out How Your Purpose

It's important to recognize what you live for, whether through creating your family's long list of meaningful moments, being a prominent figure in society, exploring new countries, doing the things on your bucket list, or something else. Knowing what drives you will help you make the right choices in life, guide your next moves, and help you grow as a person when you're running into obstacles, as well as help you lead a healthy lifestyle. Your passion will serve as a light that illuminates where you need to go and drive you forward to reach those milestones within touch!

5. Pass On The Healthy Habits To Your Family and Friends

Once you master a habit, you have the potential to pass it on to your loved ones. Then you start wondering if your friends and family could benefit from this journey as well. Suppose your family thinks that healthy foods are bland, boring, and not tasty.

Grab a delicious plant-based recipe book and chat with them about the recipes. Let them help you prepare the food, one bite at a time. You may find yourself enjoying these new dishes along with them! Don't be afraid to share on social media about your plant-based eating experience! Share your plant-based dishes for a chance to gain more than just local recognition: you may notice that other individuals are increasingly interested in breaking down their food habits and family members who will ask you for advice on how to create the best dish possible (which is a great confidence booster). No longer are people supposed to be perceived as intense critics when it comes down to eating their own words of wisdom for them - so let go of some of that tension because we all know right now it doesn't seem possible or plausible at all! But never judge a book by its cover (or a vegan/vegetarian guide by its chapters)!

6. Don't Fear To Ask For Help.

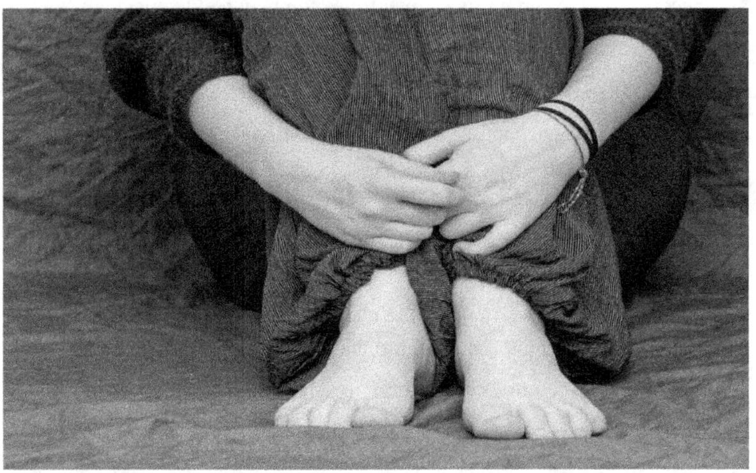

If you are suffering from any mental duress or diagnosis that may be causing you to feel unstable, we would like for you to know that there are people around who will not only accept you without prejudice but understand what it's like on your end. Loneliness is a huge risk factor when it comes to depression and anxiety – and in a lot of ways, stigma can be the culprit behind many suicides – so let us remind you that even if asking for help makes you feel insecure or embarrassing, reaching out is the best thing you can do because sometimes those with an opinion have no idea just how judgmental they sound.

CHAPTER SIXTEEN: PLANT-BASED DIET FOR THE PLANET

Is Going Plant-Based Better For The Environment?

Over the years, many people have known that eating healthy is good for helping you protect your health. But now we're starting to understand that it can do so much more! Eating a healthy, whole-food diet is not only good for your health, but it's also extremely important when it comes to living sustainably. From land use and resource allocations to the amount of pollution created by industrial-scale agricultural businesses, what you put in your mouth has a dramatic effect on the environment surrounding us all. So if you care about the death and destruction of animal farming operations across the globe as well as having a respectable impact on our planet for generations to come, then plant-based or whole foods are for you! You're welcome.

Ways In Which You Can Save The Environment By Going Plant-Based.

01.You Help Conserve Land By Going Plant-Based

Plant-based diets such as vegetarianism and veganism offer a great way to be more environment-friendly. It takes more resources to sustain an omnivorous diet.

Animals who eat plants are needed to sustain those who eat animals, and, dear goodness, that is incredibly wasteful! Adopting a plant-based dietary lifestyle does wonders for paving the way for sustainable living!

- **Growing Pastures For Livestock Causes Habitat Loss**

When animals are being reared for consumption, a common thing one may also want to keep in mind is the rate of habitat loss. In the Amazon rainforest, where there are heavy amounts of oxygen cycling and carbon dioxide regulation going on all year round, the process of ranching can account for up to 80% of deforestation.

- **Large Pieces Of Land Is Required To Grow Animal Feed**

An enormous amount of land is needed to raise animals for meat and dairy products, not to mention the space that these operations require. One of the top three uses for agricultural land in many countries is growing crops that are used as animal feed instead of being used directly as food for humans.

02.You Can Lift The Burden On Water Supply By Going Plant-Based

Water is a precious resource, taken for granted most of the time. Without water, life as we know it wouldn't exist. Sadly the effects of drought have led to record-breaking temperatures and an increase in disease and poverty worldwide. Since less than 1 percent of the earth's water is liquid freshwater, tackling water scarcity begins with a specific change: A plant-based diet.

- **Livestock Rearing Needs A Lot Of Water**

Eating animal products can be challenging to justify from a water conservation standpoint. 50 percent of the U.S. 's water consumption goes toward raising livestock - as well as poultry and pork - while only 4 percent is dedicated to fruit and veg. Animal foods also involve copious amounts of water used in their production, too: it takes an average of 1800 to 4000 gallons of water per weight or 1,800 to 4,000 gallons for every pound of beef produced. Plant proteins such as legumes have much smaller footprints, with the average footprint for each gram being six times less than that for meat.

Water footprints are used to describe the amount of water it takes to produce food through three main stages: from growing crops to making the animal feed needed to raise livestock, but they aren't just limited to livestock. There are also fish and other seafood that use an equally excessive amount of water.

- **Animal Agriculture Can Cause Water Pollution**

Animal-based agriculture is one of the leading causes of water pollution. The dairy industry can pollute bodies of water with harmful chemicals and waste. Cows and their milk are both energy-intensive to produce, can accelerate soil erosion and choke off streams in the process. Waste from industrial farm animals makes its way into surrounding waters, leading to contaminated groundwater if it's spilled over or if the waste is treated improperly. Fertilizers, pesticides, and the fuel used to farm animal feed also contribute to pollution near waterways like streams, ponds, lakes, and rivers. When too much nitrogen runoff reaches waters, it can lead to algae blooms which deplete the water of oxygen, leading all marine life in the vicinity to succumb to a slow, painful death!

03. You Can Reduce Greenhouse Gas Emissions By Going Plant-Based

Going plant-based is not just delicious and healthier; it also helps reduce greenhouse gas emissions. Be kind to the environment by going plant-based today! A new study published in the Journal of Cleaner Production found that a plant-based diet could cut global greenhouse gas emissions by 63% by 2050.

The study also found that a global shift away from the consumption of animals would also reduce the cost of environmental damage and provide economic gains of more than $1.5 trillion per year by 2050.

- **Emissions of Methane Gas Is Dangerous**

Simple choices we make can significantly reduce our environmental footprint and contribute to protecting the planet for future generations. The biggest contributors of greenhouse gases from livestock are cows, responsible for 65 percent of emissions. Raising cattle is the leading cause of methane emissions. Most cattle are ruminants; this means they naturally chew their cud (chewing again, and again, and again).

And have you ever wondered why a cow never seems to be happy? As it turns out, during digestion, cows produce methane which is about 30 times more potent than carbon dioxide in its effect on global warming! And to add insult to injury, even stored manure emits the gas too!

- **Deforestation Releases More Carbon Dioxide**

Trees breathe in carbon dioxide, and when they are cut down for lumber, furniture, and other materials, the CO_2 is released back into the air. Deforestation accounts for roughly 10 percent of all worldwide CO_2 emissions annually. This happens largely because we cut down trees to convert them into cattle pasture or clear land to grow grains fed to cows.

04.You Can Reduce Hunger In The World By Going Plant-Based

Resources that could help people around the globe are being wasted on an unnecessarily overvalued industry in animal agriculture. As it currently stands, more than 820 million people are facing a daily struggle to get enough food every day - yet some of our resources are going toward feeding animals for meat which only results in a massive waste of our collective efforts!

- **Grass-Fed Cows Even Worse!**

When considering your food choices, you may have come across the idea of grass-fed beef being a healthier and more eco-friendly option than grain-fed beef. However, that is not always the case! Cattle require a lot of land to graze on, and clearing that land destroys natural ecosystems and biodiversity. In addition, grazing animals such as cattle emit even more methane than those fed in a feedlot which is nearly three times as much, according to some research studies! You may be asking yourself, at this point, why do they do that? To answer your questions, we must consider their digestive system, or "rumination," which allows them to digest grains through fermentation.

- **Don't Forget About Seafood.**

While you may not be able to find a more heartwarming sight than a dolphin jumping out of the ocean, I want to bring your attention to something that is not so pleasant - the fact that the fishing industry is one of the most significant contributors to our oceans being choked with plastic. With discarded fishing nets alone making up around 46% of the infamous Great Pacific Garbage Patch, you would think something would be done about it! But did you know that this isn't even the worst of it? Not only are plastic nets killing off wildlife by foul means, but dolphins and whales alike are also killed in increasing numbers as bycatch. Imagine an ocean where life teems and fights for survival rather than the scars left behind by the excesses of an industry that has turned washing its hands in water a luxury within itself!

Some Critics Argue That Plant-Based Diets Aren't That Green For The Environment.

Mmm, this salad has all the savory flavors of a Mediterranean holiday. It's got lemon dressing to make it tangy, sliced almonds for crunch, and a sprinkling of cinnamon for sweetness. It is packed with nutrients as a tasty, plant-based salad to start your day. But it may be doing far less good for the planet than you'd think. This is according to some critics.

- **Avocados**

Avocados can be a great source of protein, vitamins, and fatty acids for anyone looking to adopt a plant-based diet, but one might not expect that they have such a huge impact on the environment. Trees in California require as much as 200 liters (about 46 gallons) of water every day during hot summer months; this is equivalent to filling up quite a few bathtubs! It's important to understand that avocado trees require more water than other fruit trees. This presents an environmental challenge and endangers the people and animals living in regions where wells are already running dry due to drought. This can be avoided by simply planting more trees and finding ways to conserve resources by recycling excess water – an important step that we must take if we want future generations to enjoy avocados just as much as we do!

The avocado is adapted to subtropical climates such as coastal Peru or regions of Chile, and that makes sense given the avocado's origins in coastal Mexico.

The avocado tree has relatively shallow roots, and they do not search out water held in the soil, which means they need to be continually irrigated if there is little rain. Because water usage is greater per production unit than other crops, the industry has been blamed for contributing to the chronic water shortage in some places. Avocadoes are not alone in using extreme water measures. Other fruits such as mangoes and plums take up large amounts of water too, it seems.

A kilogram of mangoes needs 686 liters of water, while the same plums need 305 liters. But fear not - there is cause for hope because some farmers claim that their 75% reduction in water usage came not from lessening their plants' length of showers but courtesy of wireless soil moisture sensors installed around their trees. The sensors monitor the ground and ensure that water is only delivered when needed - ensuring more targeted applications that use less H2O but yield just as high yield produce!

Avocados and mangos require special treatment. Their flesh is so delicate that some farmers will put them in hot water for over an hour to stop insect attacks and decay. They also ripen very quickly, which means that most of the fruit imported to Europe and the United States gets flown there by plane. The packaging and waste created during production add up to a global carbon footprint of approximately 0.55kg of CO_2 /kg for avocados and 0.6kg of CO_2 /kg for mangoes. These numbers may be lower in your country because not everyone has to airship their produce.

- **Mushrooms**

Many consider mushrooms to be a tasty and nutrient-rich option for pleasure. The University of Michigan recently found that cultivated, white button mushrooms on average produced 3kg CO_2 /kg. Researchers also found that this was less than beef which gas around 5 kg CO_2 /kg on average! But mushroom production did come out to be the same as saltwater fish and more carbonaceous than tuna, which emit 3kg/kg and 2.2 kg/ kg, respectively. Of course, overfishing is another issue altogether in need of addressing.

One further consideration is how composts are created for mushroom cultivation. Unless they're sustainably extracted from areas such as forest or manure, this can damage delicate bog ecosystems and deplete their ability to store carbon in the future.

There is a lot of hope to use more food and agricultural waste to create sustainable compost substrates for mushrooms to grow in, use the material left after harvesting to make biodegradable packaging, and piping carbon dioxide into greenhouses to grow plant-based crops will help the world become greener.

- **Mycoprotein**

Fungi to die for Mycoprotein! This superfood is a great alternative to meat, and in some cases, it is combined with egg white to have the mixture stick together. But, it may not be good for the environment too. Mycoprotein's carbon footprint is estimated to be 5.55-6.15kg CO_2 /kg by one study, but more than half of this carbon footprint comes from processing after the fungi produce the protein. Fertilizer is also needed to grow sugar the fungi feed on, accounting for 11% of the emissions.

Mycoprotein fungi can grow on agricultural food waste. Since this is a sustainable way to grow protein rather than sugar, it's no wonder why many companies are getting more interested in using more of these tiny organisms as a better alternative to other proteins out there! This could reduce the amount of carbon emitted by the process by half. Do you already have a technique to take care of that?

- **Cocoa**

It seems like cocoa, and its by-products have gotten themselves a reputation for being good for you in recent years. Sure, it's packed with antioxidants and calcium and serves as a great source of "healthy fat," but did you know that this seemingly healthful treat also comes at a price? Some argue that cocoa is also one of the biggest destroyers of the natural world, linked to tropical deforestation at an alarming rate. According to UK-based conservation group Rainforest Concern, between 1988 and 2008, an estimated 4.9 million acres of tropical forests were cleared from parts of Cote d'Ivoire, Ghana, Indonesia, and Papua New Guinea to make room for chocolate plantations. Now what's worse than that is a reported 2.1 million hectares of forest were lost to cocoa plantations between 1998-2007 alone in just West Africa! This isn't really on my bucket list.

There are many chocolate lovers in the world. But before you indulge in the tasty treat, you might want to think about where it came from. Tropical rainforests may seem like harmless wooded areas with nothing but trees, wildlife, and rivers -- but there is much more to them than that! Because tropical forests absorb a large amount of carbon dioxide in the air and give off oxygen, deforestation can cause a major shift in global climates. And that isn't nice for us all. Even worse is how cocoa farms often turn rainforests into deserts

Animal products typically have a higher carbon footprint than plant-based foods because livestock produces large emissions every year. Vegan consumers can receive more information on how their food was produced and its impact on the environment to help them make better choices at the supermarket if they want to reduce their carbon footprint.

- **Almonds and cashew nuts**

We all love nuts. They can be enjoyed in a variety of ways and are very versatile. Some of the most valuable nuts on Earth include almonds, cashews, and walnuts. These nuts are packed with proteins, minerals, and other essential nutrients; we definitely could not live without them, but so that you know - they happen to consume far more water than others on this list. Unlike many other crop types that you can find in the supermarket (think corn, soybeans, etc.), tree nuts require significant amounts of water and special fertilizers and pesticides to grow. As a result, these crops have a huge impact on the environment because they take over three times more freshwater for each kilo of a shelled nut than some other crops. Research shows us that the amount of water required by almonds is more than that needed for any other crop.

You Can Make Your Plant-Based Diet Eco-friendly.

Living a plant-based lifestyle is the best way to make sure you put less of a strain on the environment. If you have the option, why not choose unprocessed foods from local farmers? When you do buy your fruits and veggies (even packaged in biodegradable, compostable packaging), ensure that they're seasonal produce so that you aren't shipping food thousands of miles for no reason! Lastly, buy only what you can eat, so it doesn't go to waste.

Estimates say one-third of the food in North America ends up as waste when nobody eats it; so don't let your groceries go from fun little bunches of yellow peppers to sad little bunches of moldy and smelly green peppers just because you didn't bother taking them out of the grocery sack before going to bed!

These Documentaries Can Change The Way You Eat And Help You Adopt A Plant-Based Lifestyle

I.   Our Planet

Our Planet is an all-new series narrated by David Attenborough, premiered on Netflix in 2019. The show educates us about our planet and animals, mostly with beautiful footage of amazing animals from their natural surroundings. However, this time around, the focus tends to be more on the impact humans have on the environment than ever before seen in nature documentaries as it does not only take a look at how climate change impacts all creatures that roam upon this Earth but also how we are such culprits of its motives. It's also important to note that you can benefit animals by doing your best to cut down on trash in your life. Recycle when possible, use reusable bags when shopping, or even purchase things from companies that use environmentally friendly packaging. Also, remember: if you're considering adopting an animal, please adopt one from your local shelter!

II.   Forks Over Knives

The documentary Forks Over Knives can help people understand how going plant-based may reverse certain chronic diseases and the steps they need to take to start living longer and healthier lives. Exploring new cures and developing high-tech solutions is great. Still, sometimes we have to look deeper, which is why taking a fresh look at old ways of putting food back into our bodies as medicine is causing quite a stir in scientific and medical communities around the globe. It is based on the leading-edge research of T. Colin Campbell, Ph.D., and Caldwell Esselstyn, MD.

III.   The Invisible Vegan

In the Invisible Vegan documentary, viewers learn more about the struggles and lifestyles of African-American communities. The filmmaker, Jasmine Leyva, shares her story about growing up in a household with unhealthy eating patterns and little nutritional information accessible to her. Leyva is committed to helping others create better health decisions through her research and education efforts.

IV.   Food, Inc.

Food, Inc. is a 2009 documentary by filmmaker Robert Kenner. It's an interesting documentary that examines all how corporations have integrated into the food chain in America. Food Inc. shows us examples of what happens when profit is put before public health and how little regard companies have for farmers, safety, and the environment. Because of this film, there has been a dramatic increase in people thinking about their diets and making healthier choices when it comes to food—even if it means only eating vegetarian or vegan!

V.   Seaspiracy

When it comes to our oceans, you could say that we're a bit like Adam and Eve. We both live on the same planet, but one lives in the Land of Knowledge while the other lingers in the Land of Obliviousness. The ones living in the land of obliviousness don't seem to be aware that by wiping out vast parts of our oceans, they are destroying their natural habitats and subsequently threatening almost all sea life, including themselves. It's a fact that most people don't know. Still, they need to learn, so we're very glad a few people out there have introduced documentaries such as Seaspiracy, which shows exactly why it should be everyone's top priority!

Seaspiracy, released in 2021, seeks to educate its viewers on how the world's oceans are affected. Filmmakers Ali and Lucy Tabrizi travel across the globe to see how our consumption habits and government policies affect ocean life.

Throughout their journey, they discover that while government policies, overfishing, and even certain environmental groups' actions can devastate marine life, those same resources can contribute to the ocean's protection.

VI.   Meet Me Halfway

We realize not everyone will go full vegan overnight, and that's okay! Everyone's at a different place in their journey, and we want to respect the fact that making steps towards a more compassionate diet is a good thing. The important thing to keep in mind is that you don't have to cut out meat altogether to make your diet more "vegan." If you cut back from three meals per week with meat as the center of the meal, these calories can be replaced by plant-based protein sources. Let's say, for example, that traditional breakfast for one has two slices of bacon on top of an egg scramble. Instead of this high protein animal-based meal, it might be possible to start with toast or oatmeal instead (no added bacon here!), and won't this still give us all of the same nutrients? Certainly, there will be no bacon taste or texture lost by switching over; rather, we are just getting healthier while aiding the environment!

The Meet me Halfway documentary breaks the assumption of veganism being some homogeneous movement. Instead, it shows how individuals are stretching this "meaty" term to ensure that even meat-eaters can participate in a reduction strategy and reap the benefits of green products and companies. The film highlights not just Kateman's experience with eating less meat but also the many skilled entrepreneurs who use ingenuity to create a demand for environmentally conscious alternatives such as those found on FARM USA.

VII.   EARTHLINGS

EARTHLINGS is an inspiring documentary about our relationship with animals. The film covers five topics: pets, food, clothing, entertainment (zoos and circuses), scientific research, and animal experimentation. It's narrated by: Oscar-winning actor Joaquin Phoenix (Gladiator), features music by Moby (the director's cousin), and was written and directed by Shaun Monson.

VIII.   Eating You Alive

Science is developing rapidly, helping us find cures and treatments for diseases that once were thought to be fatal. However, unfortunately, those suffering from chronic disease are still dying of stroke and obesity daily. Eating You Alive takes on a deeper look into the mystery of why there's no solution or protection against aggressive diseases such as heart disease, diabetes, and even cancer - diseases that previously were thought to be incurable! We've become so conditioned to look towards science for answers in today's world, but are we overlooking the most powerful medicine known to man? A plant-based diet has been scientifically proven to reverse and prevent these ailments without harmful side effects and without taking any risks with your life. Why aren't more doctors preaching what they know is true if it could improve their patient's health?

IX.   Cowspiracy

Have you ever wondered how the size of our large-scale animal farms affects the world around us? Cowspiracy takes an in-depth look into the impact such massive numbers of livestock have had on some vital resources like water, forests, and lakes across our planet. From deforestation, drinking water pollution, and greenhouse gases all caused by large-scale animal farming, it seems that these major industries are trying to hide their responsibility for all the harm they have caused to make a profit!

X.   What The Health?

What The Health is the Forks Over Knives film you didn't ask for, but maybe thank yourself for watching in the end. This controversial documentary argues that many of the same points while exposing a major conflict of interest between media sources and medical/pharmaceutical establishments because their ties to Big Food so heavily compromise them.

XI.   The Game Changers

The Game Changers documentary examines the performance-enhancing benefits of The Earthlings plant-based diet, which is a groundbreaking way to increase human strength. We follow James Wilks—a former Special Forces trainer and winner of the MMA show The Ultimate Fighter—as he gathers and absorbs new knowledge about nutrition and how it can affect his body in many ways that promote optimal performance.

XII.   An Inconvenient Truth

Climate Change is one of the most discussed phenomena in our contemporary society. An Inconvenient Truth - released in 2006, produced by Lawrence Bender, Scott Burns, and Davis Guggenheim - is a documentary that helped ignite the movement around people becoming aware of how human activity has put our environment under threat.

The fact-based film tells a compelling story about one man's battle to bring awareness to the general public about the dangerous effects of global warming and how it is poised to harm all of us and our planet if it is not addressed immediately. What we learn from this documentary, however, is that there are many ways we can address climate change and lessen its harmful effects so long as we work together globally to make sure these issues are confronted before they escalate further still.

XIII.   Kiss the Ground

Whether you are a champion of wildlife for ethical or environmental reasons or a well-intentioned urban farmer, perhaps you've had an "aha moment" after watching Netflix's latest documentary: Kiss the Ground. The film follows author and journalist Jeff Brown's journey into what many consider the future of agriculture—regenerative farming—which turns carbon pollution into topsoil that can heal our planet and reverse the course of climate change. Although we love our local farmers' markets, the food system contributes more greenhouse emissions than every plane, ship, train, bus, truck, and car in the world combined. So engaging are Kook's talks with an expert ensemble (including vegan actor Woody Harrelson).

We might agree with Harrelson's sentiment that identifying as an environmentalist should no longer be enough - we all need to be regenerative activists!

XIV.   Eating Animals

This documentary, Eating Animals, released in 2018, gives viewers an inside look at the evolution of animal agriculture into the industrial process it has become today. It explores the environmental, economic, and public health issues tied to factory farming, as well as delving into the use of antibiotics and hormones.

XV.   Gunda

When you think about it, many of us don't understand animals. I mean, we know how to care for a lot of different creatures according to their needs, but are we prepared to establish contact with them? Have you ever heard of Gunda? Yes, that's a sow, and if you want to watch an amazing animal documentary named after her - then GUNDA is the one for you! It tells the story of what it means to experience life as an animal, how far our moral compass can reach yet, and whether we're able to share our planet with billions of other people. If not, why? This is a truly remarkable cinematic achievement - Victor Kossakovsky made us all think in this breathtaking documentary!

XVI.   PLANEAT

PLANEAT is a documentary so heart-warming and thoughtful that it could even change how you eat forever. If indeed, you are tired of feeling tired, having trouble losing weight, or suffering from a chronic disease, then you may want to watch a film that explores the link between diet and disease, as revealed by Dr. T Colin Campbell's decades-long study. The many benefits of following Dr. Casselberry Esselstyn's plant-based diet will be sure to help you regain your health, especially if you happen to have suffered strokes or heart attacks in the past. At PLANEAT, we also invite you to watch Prof Gidon Eshel's compelling research, which demonstrates how certain food choices have severe effects on our environment and the world around us, as we saw during this documentary which follows these outstanding scientists throughout their years-long studies and experiments that finally culminated in PLANEAT: The Movie!

What You'll Gain From These Documentaries

Documentaries are like desserts. They're enjoyable, inspiring, and delightful to consume, not to mention that they do a lot of good with their audiences. Ask your friends who haven't seen them what their favorite movie is - and once you finish telling them about this documentary, you've found that's all about the importance of adopting a delicious plant-based diet full of nutrients, the health benefits it has for you both physically and mentally, some tasty recipes to try out, meal plans that may aid in your transition period and a checklist for important implementation steps to keep everything organized, see if they'll watch it with you!

CONCLUSION

Thanks again for purchasing this book and congratulations for reading it till the end.

While it is never too late to change your diet, it is natural to feel a bit overwhelmed when first starting out. It is important to remember that you can take your time and enjoy learning about the different plant-based diets and plant-based recipes. With the right information, you will have the tools you need to make eating healthier a part of your daily routine.

I hope this book on plant-based diet eating guides for the middle-aged has been helpful for you. Setting up a plant-based diet is easier than you think, and you'll find that it actually makes losing weight easier and improves your athletic performance sex life than what you're used to! You can also take the necessary steps to ensure that you contribute positively to climate change because this planet is our home; not forgetting that adopting a plant-based diet is the best dietary intervention for your health. We all deserve to live a peaceful and healthy life.

Finally, if you enjoyed this book, please let me know your thoughts with a short review on Amazon. All that you need to do is to click the blue link next to the yellow stars that says "customer reviews." You'll then see a gray button that says "Write a customer review"—click that and you're good to go. It means a lot, thank you!

Edyth

While all attempts have been made to verify the information provided in this publication, neither the author nor the publisher assumes any responsibility for errors, omissions, contrary interpretations of the subject matter herein, or liability whatsoever on behalf of the purchaser or reader of these materials.